Management

Is This Any Way to Run a Company?

Read One Short Chapter a Day and
Be a Better Manager the Next Morning

By

H. Lee Rust

Florida Corporate Finance
322 E. Central Blvd. #1001
Orlando, FL 32801

(407) 841-5676
hleerust@att.net

Is This Any Way to Run a Company?

Printed in the U.S.A. by Lulu.com

To contact the author please call Florida Corporate Finance at (407) 841-5676 or e-mail: hleerust@att.net.

Florida Corporate Finance
322 E. Central Blvd. #1001
Orlando, FL 32801

Library of Congress Control Number: 2008903781

Rust, H. Lee
    Is This Any Way to Buy a Company? / by H. Lee Rust
        p. cm.
    Includes index
    ISBN: 978-0-615-20584-7 (paper)

        1. Business Management, 2. Management - General,
        3. Business Operations, 4. Small Business, 5. Business.

1

Is This Any Way to Run a Company?

*Read One Short Chapter a Day and
Be a Better Manager the Next Morning*

Contents

2

Is This Any Way to Run a Company?   H. Lee Rust

3

Is This Any Way to Run a Company?   H. Lee Rust

Is This Any Way to Run a Company?

Read One Short Chapter a Day and
Be a Better Manager the Next Morning

Introduction

Through most of your life, you've been told to learn from your mistakes. It's more fun, however, and often more productive to learn from the mistakes of others; then you don't have to make them yourself. That's particularly true in business where mistakes can be costly and, on occasion, even fatal.

In this book, we'll explore a wide variety of corporate management topics. Many will describe mistakes made by some of my corporate finance clients over the years and what they did to correct those mistakes. In cases where they did nothing, or even the wrong thing, we'll also explore the consequences and what could have been done better.

All of the management problems, suggestions, and solutions presented in this book are real-life examples. They happened to people like you facing the same business problems you face. As a result, this book is long on experience and short on theory.

Most business owners and executives don't need an exhaustive Harvard Business School case study on a single subject. They need practical advice they can digest in a few minutes and put to work now. They need advice from the real world of real people facing the same challenges they face every day. This book provides that advice.

You see your company (or your client's companies if you're an attorney, accountant, or consultant) only through your own eyes, but you can benefit from the insight of others. Smart people on occasion do stupid things. We can look at some of those stupid things and perhaps avoid making the same errors.

Some of the chapters in this book will be short, only a few paragraphs; some will be longer. A hundred years or so ago, a classical author in a letter to a friend said, "If I had more time, I would have made this letter shorter." Following that advice, I'll try to say what needs to be said quickly and succinctly.

Often I'll use examples taken from the years I've spent working with the owners and executives of what were usually small and mid-sized companies. Those examples relate to efforts by the managers at those companies to improve financial results, expand their operations, or increase the returns from their investments of time and money.

5

Some people succeed in spite of themselves, but it happens only rarely. Most company owners and executives succeed because they do the right things or, at least, they do them more frequently than the wrong things. When they do something wrong, they recognize the mistake, do something to change it, and then measure the results.

From time to time, my father, who was a brilliant businessman, told me, "The motto for the day is: Do something, even if it's wrong." Doing nothing is seldom the correct answer; making an attempt is almost always better. An attempt based on past experience, whether your own or someone else's, is better yet.

So lets look at... "Is this any way to run a company?" Sometimes the answer will be "no"; sometimes it will be "yes", but in all cases, the answer should be instructive.

However one word of caution. There are many topics covered in this book. You can't and shouldn't attempt to either embrace them all or even a majority. You must know what will be best for you and for your company. In addition, if you make too many changes too quickly you can't measure the results of only one or a few. Instead, you should proceed slowly, be sure any change made was the correct one, and only then explore others. Prioritize your action list

As you read this book, you might also want to remember another of my father's sayings:

> *I know you believe you understood what you think I said, but*
> *I'm not sure you realize that what you heard is not what I meant.*

I hope you enjoy reading this book as much as I enjoyed writing it. I also hope it makes you a better manager without the tedious theories from business school curricula that might not apply to your immediate business problems.

6

Chapter 1 - Fire Some Customers

Here's a radical idea: Fire some of your customers. Most company executives and managers spend a significant amount of time attempting to increase their customer base by selling more stuff to more people. They never think that some of those customers, including some they've had for years, may be unprofitable. Get rid of those and sales will go down, but profits will go up.

Several years ago, I did some strategic planning for a small steel fabrication shop. Their largest customer was particularly demanding, not only as to deliveries and quality but as to prices as well. That customer never missed an opportunity to demand a price cut. Because it represented over thirty percent of the company's annual sales, both the shop owner and the sales manager continued to surrender to those price demands. That company filed for bankruptcy reorganization and was eventually liquidated.

At the time, I also happened to be involved with the fab shop that took over that demanding customer and part of its fabrication business. At the start of that relationship, they sat down with the customer and went through a comprehensive list of each component to be manufactured.

They raised prices in varying amounts for every piece. When the customer replied that they could buy an item cheaper from another supplier, the answer was, "Fine, you should do that." That company still manufacturers the majority, but not all, of those parts and generates profits not only on the work for that customer but also for their company as a whole.

There are a number of reasons why you might consider firing a customer. For example, if you deal with a company that is chronically late paying your invoices, you should ask to review a copy of their financial statements. If those late payments result from a poor financial condition, don't worry about the effect on your revenue of losing that customer. Think instead about the effect of taking a bad debt loss on their entire receivable. You can't afford to deal with a customer who might not pay at all.

However, if that customer's financial condition does not appear unduly weak, simply tell them that you want a written agreement as to extended payment terms. Then calculate your cost of carrying that receivable beyond thirty days and add that cost to the prices charged that customer. If they don't want to accept the price increase, ask that they pay on time. Your company is not a bank for your customers. (Unless, of course, it is indeed a bank.)

By the way, if a customer with a history of late payments will not give you their financial statements, that should be enough reason to consider firing them.

7

Most managers have heard many times that "twenty percent of your customers will usually represent over eighty percent of your annual sales." If that's the case with your company, it might be wise to investigate the profitability of servicing the large number of small buyers. If the cost of maintaining a customer relationship is too high in relation to the revenues and gross profits generated, perhaps that customer should be fired or the prices raised.

In addition to a customer demanding a price cut that makes its business unprofitable, there are other customer demands that can result in a de facto price cut and the elimination of profits for that individual account. Among those are continual backcharges due to real or perceived quality issues or other reasons the customer might use to pay less than the invoiced amount. In addition, if a customer's demands or delivery requirements result in constant overtime work, the increased production costs will reduce the profitability of that account, perhaps to zero or below.

Delivery costs for a remote customer should also be included in their pricing calculations. Those delivery costs are as real as the costs for direct labor and materials. If the delivery costs exceed the profitability for an account, you shouldn't continue to serve that customer. I recently had a client whose company produces a heavy product with a low gross margin. In order to service a large and important customer throughout an area that includes cities beyond their profitable shipping radius, they found co-packers who would gladly private label materials and ship to that customer in their markets. The customer is happy, and my client's company is more profitable.

The rule is simple: If an account isn't profitable, you shouldn't have it. Why pay your customer for the privilege of servicing their account? Rather than lose money servicing any customer, let your competitors do that. Your company will be stronger, and your competitors will be weaker.

Of course, price and profits are not the only consideration in a customer relationship. Some people are simply too ornery to deal with; a chronically unpleasant customer is one which should be suspect.

At least once a year, every business owner or other appropriate executives should review with their sales managers their entire customer list. Fire those who shouldn't be on the list. The objective is not to maximize revenues; the objective is to maximize profits. And don't forget the old cliché: you can't make up for losses by increasing your sales of products priced below costs.

8

Chapter 2 - Hire Good People

"Surround yourself with good people. Give them a well defined job to do. Then get out of the way, and let 'em do it." That was another piece of good advice I received from my father years ago. He built a highly successful engineering/construction company by hiring talented people and giving them both the responsibility and authority to make their own decisions. "Why would I hire someone," he explained, "if I can do the job better than they can."

I had a client not long ago in the electrical contracting business. He had built a company of some size and scope including several acquisitions of remote facilities. The company had long outgrown its original bookkeeper. In searching for a more talented person, my client ended up with two choices. One was a comptroller who would require an annual salary in the $45,000 range. Another was a significantly more talented CFO at about $100,000.

Even though the company could easily afford the more expensive person, my client, against my advice, hired the comptroller. Over time, the delay in producing the financial statements climbed to forty-five days after each month's close. The project and profit center accounting was both wrong and useless for control purposes. The accounting manager was overextended in a job more complex than any he had faced in the past. There were, however, always reasons to keep this unqualified person, not the least of which was the difficulty in developing a euphemism for "You're fired".

Finally, the company's principal bank made the decision by accelerating its loans and asked my client to find another banking relationship. The reason was simple; the bank could no longer trust the company's financial reports. Hidden in those late and inaccurate statements was the fact that the company was insolvent. My client was an accomplished electrician, not an accountant. One person, one bad hire, brought that company to the brink of bankruptcy. That's an extreme example of making bad hiring choices, but it can and will happen again in other companies.

I've also had clients who promoted their best salesperson to sales manager. As a result, they lost their best salesman and got a mediocre sales manager. Although some salespeople might make an excellent sales manager, some won't. Be sure you know the difference. In promoting as well in hiring new employees, surround yourself with as many people as you can find who are more talented than you. (Also see Chapter 7.)

Once you have those talented people in place, if you then try to tell them how to do their jobs, maybe you don't need them. If you expect them to do their jobs the way you would do them, you won't get any new ideas. Great

9

suggestions may be stifled. Years ago, I saw a cartoon that showed a company owner at the head of a table surrounded by his management team. He was saying, "All in favor say 'Yes'; all opposed say 'I resign'." That was a man destined to forever run a company that would generate results near the bottom of its industry.

If you surround yourself with people more talented than you, however, you will have accomplished only a part of your job. In addition, you must give those managers clear directions as to their jobs and your expectations. Then let them do their jobs with a minimum of interference. But don't forget that you must also give them the ability to measure their own progress toward well defined goals. No one can control what they can't measure.

The majority of company executives and managers seem to believe there's some mystique to their financial statements. They guard them closely with access limited to only them, their bankers, and their accounting staff. Why? Public companies report their financial results quarterly to all the world, and it doesn't seem to hurt them. If you want to maximize your company's profits, give each profit center manager the accounting data he or she needs to control their operations, to set goals, and to measure their performance toward those goals. If you want your profit center managers to cooperate and make decisions that contribute to the welfare of the entire company, give them the entire company's financial statements. (Also see Chapter 8.)

If your managers know how profitable the company is, they'll be proud. If you're afraid that knowledge will lead to higher salary demands, perhaps you aren't paying enough. And if you listen only to your own ideas, you'll be getting severely limited advice from a narrow base of experience. Hire the best talent you can afford, pay them well, and listen to what they have to say. Your company will prosper. (Also see Chapter 27.)

Chapter 3 - Call Yourself

G o out today and place a phone call to yourself or have someone else do it for you. You might be surprised by the results.

In most companies, one of the lowest paid and least trained of the employees is the first contact an outsider has with the company: its telephone receptionist. How your phone is answered and the exchange that follows can influence a caller's attitude toward your company and its products or services. Why not be sure that attitude and initial impression is positive?

First, the receptionist should slow down and speak both calmly and clearly. Answering a phone

"wilsonjonesandsmithhowcanidirectyourcall"

is not helpful. You and your receptionist should be proud of your company's name. When someone calls, be sure that it is accentuated and not hidden in a jumble of words that no one can either follow or understand.

Also, your receptionist should never interrupt a caller. How often have you had this exchange: "Could I please speak with Bill Williams; this is...." "Can-I-tell-him-who's-calling?"

And don't put callers on hold forever. Your receptionist should ask if he or she might put the caller on hold. Then let the caller know within thirty seconds if there will be a delay, if the other party is on another call, or if the person being called must be paged. A caller shouldn't wonder if the call has been disconnected, if there is anyone at the company other than the receptionist, or if the receptionist has decided to leave for lunch.

Of course, being on hold, whether short or long, is even worse when faced with raucous music that is both inappropriate and loud. Any music on your phone system should be designed specifically for office "on-hold" use and should be both soft and unobtrusive.

The worst is to tap a radio station into your office phone for on-hold use. Have you ever been on hold when an advertisement for laxatives or personal lubricants suddenly came on the radio station that is being forced on you as you wait? Do you really want "Cop Killer Rap" to represent your company to a caller?

How often have you been on a long hold and had a recorded voice say repeatedly, "We value your call...." If you value my call, don't let me sit through the recording sixteen times.

In particular, don't put any caller into a endless loop where it's impossible to reach a live person. If you use extensions without a receptionist, just make sure your phone system always responds to dialing "0" and has a person who

11

will always answer. If the primary receptionist is not at his or her desk, the call should automatically transfer to someone who will answer. The inability to talk with anyone who is not a recorded or computer generated voice is not only madding but also a poor presentation of your concern for people trying to contact your company.

Your telephone receptionist should also realize that he or she does not have all the answers and should not speak for the company on major corporate issues. On occasion, I've called companies and explained that I am a corporate finance consultant representing a company available for acquisition that might be of interest to XYZ Corp. After asking to whom I should speak, the receptionist has responded, "We wouldn't be interested in that." As I hung up and crossed that company off my list, I wondered how an hourly paid receptionist could make that decision for the company. Oh well, others were certainly interested.

As you study your phone system and the response your company gives a caller, also ask yourself how accessible you are. Unless you're the CEO of a multi-billion company, answer your desk phone yourself. After I've responded to the questions posed by a receptionist and then reached an assistant only to answer them again and then had the assistant ask, "Can I tell him what this call is about?", I want to respond, "Yes, this is the Pink Pussycat Motel. We wanted to tell him he left his American Express card on our water bed." If I wanted to talk with an assistant, I would have asked for the assistant when I first called.

It's also important that you choose your receptionist with care. Do you really want someone with the personality of a bear trap being the first contract anyone has with your company? We all have bad days on occasion, but some have bad days every day. Make sure one of those is not answering your company's phone.

As a last little note, you should also place your calls yourself. It doesn't happen often, but I've received calls with the greeting, "Mr. Wilson is calling; just a minute please." As I'm waiting for Mr. Wilson, I think how pretentious and egotistical he must be.

Think about the first contact the world has with your company and be sure the impression given is the one you want to represent your entire organization. Make sure your telephone receptionists are well trained, know what to say as well as what is inappropriate, and treat callers with the patience and respect you would want to receive. You can't know if that's done without either calling yourself or having someone else call you to report on the reception they receive.

Chapter 4 - The Internet and Your Company

I recently had to buy a desk phone for my office, but I didn't get in my car and drive to the mall. I went to the internet where the selection was larger, the prices were lower, and detailed information on the various models was better. If you don't think that both the internet and social media has changed the way the world does business, ask a teenager. They are the customers and business managers of the future.

Today, every business should have a website and should use it as a marketing tool as well as a means of communicating with its customers, suppliers, and employees. If your website is only an online brochure, it needs to be radically updated. If it already has some interactive and communications features, they should be reviewed and also updated. If you don't have an effective website, your business is operating at a distinct disadvantage regardless of the markets you serve. (Also see Chapter 40.)

First, make sure your website has effective, pleasing, and appropriate graphics. Then make sure it's easy to navigate with a logical sequence of pages and the means to access them. And finally, make sure it has all of the information needed as an introduction to anyone interested in your company, its products, or its services. That should certainly include your address and phone number and the e-mail addresses for your top officers and managers.

A few months ago, I wanted to contact Georgia-Pacific Corporation, one of the major pulp, paper, and lumber companies in the U.S. I was surprised to find that their voluminous website has no address or phone number for the corporate headquarters or for any other of their operations. The only "Contact Us" link accesses a blank e-mail form that would send a message to "info@". That wasn't what I needed.

In addition to being informative, your website should also be interactive to the maximum extent possible. If you are in a business that sells a product, your website should have order-on-line capabilities with an immediate link to your order fulfillment department. For every order, the site should provide the customer with an e-mail confirmation within minutes of the order. It should also have a method of checking the status of an order, a shipping date and method, and tracking information after shipment.

One of my recent clients was reluctant to provide a product sales function on her company's website. She reasoned that she didn't want to compete with her customers, the numerous retail stores which sold her company's scuba equipment. She solved that problem by adding the sales function but automatically forwarding each order from the website to the nearest retail store

13

for packing and shipping. This website function then became a sales tool when recruiting new retail outlets. It also relieved my client's company of the fulfillment obligations and cost while getting the order to the customer faster.

Your website is particularly important if your products require replacement parts. To promote and increase your sales of these high margin parts, add schematic drawings to your website. Those drawings should show expanded views of your equipment with each part identified. Any customer should then be able to order a part using only a mouse click on either the part number or the drawing.

To see how this can work, go to www.toro.com/parts. Under the "PartsTree" section click on various items and look at the detailed schematics. From the Toro site, a parts order can be routed directly to the distributor nearest your location. Your company may not have either the number of equipment items or complexity of Toro turf equipment, but that little exercise can give you an idea of how you can help your customers, add to your parts sales, and provide a convenience your competitors might not yet offer.

If you are in a service business, your company's site should give potential and existing customers a portal into those services. A potential customer should be able to request a quotation for a specific service or ask an e-mail question regarding your services directly from the site. In addition, an existing customer might, for example, have password protected access to the schedule for their project, links for e-mails to the various participants in the project, and methods for checking project costs to date and estimates for costs to complete.

If your company is a contractor, password protected access to a wide variety of project information should be available, including schedules for major segments of the project; change order submissions, status, and approval functions; key material and equipment order status; and invoice status for past and outstanding billings. The website could also include project specifications, project drawings, and a particularly easy method of accessing other project specific information for customers, project supervision personnel, subcontractors, and suppliers. The ability of both suppliers and subcontractors to download CAD/CAM engineering drawings from the site can be a particularly effective and inexpensive method of delivering that information.

In virtually any business, its website can also be used as an effective tool for communicating with your employees. A monthly employee newsletter should be posted on the site with one person in your company responsible for the monthly updates and for posting interesting articles written by others. For its interactive function, you should provide a means of receiving comments from your employees (a form of electronic suggestion box) and a method of responding using their e-mail addresses. Employee safety and other training tools could be presented as an alternate to class room participation with methods of both testing and monitoring attendance. Your entire employee

14

handbook and your management procedure manuals should be on the site with password protected access limited to specific people or classes of employees.

As a recruiting tool, a corporate website can be a particularly effect method of advising site visitors of employment opportunities in your company. Interested individuals should be able to complete an employment application and submit it directly from the site followed by an e-mail confirmation of receipt by your company. The applicant should also receive an indication of when the appropriate person will respond to their application.

In most cases, your site should also have a Spanish language option and, depending upon the extent of your foreign markets, other languages which can be chosen with the click of a mouse.

By the way, how often have you wanted to print a web page only to find the words on the right hand of the printed page are beyond the margin and can't be read? A quick fix may be to click on "File" at the top left of your computer screen, then "Page Setup", and then choose "Landscape" under "Orientation". Then when you print the page, all the words will be there but the page will be turned 90 degrees.

In addition, for your website, don't make your visitors go through this exercise even if they know what to do. If a visitor to your site wants to print any page, make sure it can be printed in full without any manual changes.

In today's business world, your website is one of the most important communication tools for any person who might want to contact your company. That includes anyone who needs to know more about your products or services, express a concern, or otherwise interact with key people in your organization.

By updating your website and expanding its use, you can convert what is often a neglected and outdated online catalog into a substantial competitive advantage. If you don't do this, your competitors will. Start by listing all of the categories of people with whom your company communicates. Then add the form of those communications for each category. You can then review that list for functions that could or should be added to your website. Make your Company's website the most complete and comprehensive in your industry. You'll be rewarded for the effort.

Chapter 5 - Simplify Your Financial Statements

On occasion, I've been asked what I think is the greatest failing at many if not most small and med-sized companies. That's easy. The answer is inadequate internal financial controls. The reason is also simple. Entrepreneurs start most companies, and entrepreneurs are seldom accountants. The result at the majority of private companies is a lack of knowledge of accounting principals by the owners and key managers. They seldom understand how financial data can be used to improve their company, contribute to its growth, or solve operating problems that aren't necessarily related to accounting matters.

As a result of this general deficiency, we'll address accounting issues in a number of places in this book. (In particular, see Chapters 44 and 45.) Let's start by examining what you and your comptroller or CFO can do to make your financial statements easier to both read and use. The general format for most financial statements is established by a company's accounting manager based on software constraints, audit or annual review needs, tax reporting requirements, and General Accepted Accounting Principals or GAAP. None of those, however, specifically address the needs of the company's management for control information. That can and should be changed. Because your managers are not accountants, start by working with your accounting manager to drastically reduce the number of line items and pages included in the monthly statements given to your managers.

None of the managers care how much the company spends on payroll taxes. Those taxes are always a set percentage of wages up to certain levels. The important information regarding all elements of compensation is only the total cost of employing the people in certain departments. It is not a breakdown between payroll, payroll taxes, and employee benefits. Combine all employee compensation expenses into a single line item for each department that should be monitored.

For instance, you might have a single Employee Compensation line for Selling Expense and another for G&A Costs. Each of those should consolidate wages, payroll taxes, health benefits, vacation and holiday pay, and pension plan costs. The total compensation line items might also include workers' compensation premiums. Those premiums, however, should be kept separate for your production, field personnel, or others for whom that insurance is both a significant cost and controllable.

This same principal of line item consolidation can also be used to report Occupancy Costs combining rent, utilities, security monitoring, trash removal, landscaping, and property taxes. Vehicle Expense might include employee mileage allowances, oil and gas, general auto repairs, tag expense, and vehicle insurance. In considering such consolidations, ask yourself what information is important for either operating controls or an understanding of how your business functions.   Do you really need a depreciation charge breakdown between buildings, equipment, and vehicles?   If not, combine them into a single Depreciation line item.

Then determine what minimum annual expense is pertinent to your operations. I've had clients with companies grossing $20 million in annual sales who report some individual line items of less than $100 per year. That can't be important to an understanding of the company's performance or for controlling that performance. Set a minimum amount for any separate line item and combine all expenses of less than that amount into a related line item or in the Miscellaneous Costs category.

To do all of this, sit down with your accounting manager and go through several monthly financial statements.   Determine which items should be consolidated and which are important as either business information or as control tools. Once the consolidation is completed, however, you should still have the ability within your accounting software to expand any line item that shows unusual change or raises questions.   In most cases, your income statements should not be more than a single page for each department or profit center and no more than two pages for the consolidated monthly statements.

As a part of reducing your income statements and balance sheets to a minimum number of lines, also make sure that the business segments, departments, or categories which are reported separately match those you need for an understanding of how your company functions. I've seen monthly financial statements that show individual G&A Expense line items of less than .005% of annual sales but then show Cost of Goods Sold on only a single line at 65% of sales.

If any expense category should be divided among its constituent parts, Cost of Goods Sold should be at the top of the list. Your control over these critical production or service related expenses largely determines the profitability of your company, not whether General Liability Insurance cost $2,000 or $2,100 dollars last month.   Your Costs of Goods Sold or Direct Costs reporting category should include individual lines for Direct Labor, Material, and Other Direct Costs.   Then use additional lines for any items that are particularly important to your business such as Outgoing Freight, Repairs & Maintenance, Production Supplies, or other such direct costs that should be monitored as a percent of Total Sales.

In addition to this Direct Cost category, also make sure you have divided your operations into individual profit centers for which you can, and should, hold the department managers responsible. In certain cases, this departmental profit center accounting will require establishing a number of intercompany transfer prices.

17

I recently had a client whose company manufactures products which are then sold through her own stores. She thought she was running each store as a profit center. However, she was pricing the products she transferred to the stores at cost. As a result, she could not measure the "profits" generated by the manufacturing operations and was overstating the profitability of the individual stores. By establishing internal transfer pricing at market rates, she solved both of those problems. She also used the profit center information for a new performance-based bonus program that increased the profits generated by both the manufacturing operations and the stores.

Also, don't use your financial statements to lie to yourself. Several years ago, I had a client who manipulated his project percent complete numbers each month as a means of smoothing his profits as the year progressed. He thought it looked better to his bank not to have wide swings in his monthly results. He didn't realize that those swings were due to widely different profits (or losses) being generated by individual projects. He had given up project cost accounting to kid both himself and his bankers. That company soon disappeared in a bankruptcy sale.

You don't have to be an accountant to understand what your financial statements tell you, but you and other members of your management team must be able to quickly and easily read and interpret them. All of you should then be able to use the accounting information to better control your operations. If you don't think your managers can read an income statement, base a quarterly bonus on the results those statements report. They'll quickly learn to interpret the reported results, and both your company's profits and the managers' compensation will go up.

18

Chapter 6 - Sales & Selling

You might be amazed at how many of my clients' companies have but a single sales technique. They answer the telephone. Someone calls to say they want to buy a widget or a certain service and the response is, "Oh yes, we make those," or, "Oh yes, we do that." Their only active sales work is to rely on their reputation, their past relationships, and the "word-of-mouth" system of sales. While those might suffice to maintain a modest level of revenues, they won't contribute much to growth, adequate market penetration, or an operation of significant size,

Many company owners know little of sales and marketing techniques. The reason is simple: most entrepreneurs are better versed in the products they manufacture or the services they provide than how to sell those products or services. They gained their experience making things or doing things and, in many cases, not in selling those things. Once your company is established, however, any owner or principal operating executive should turn their attention to sales and marketing.

Although the words "sales and marketing" are most frequently presented as a single subject, marketing is quite different from sales. (For an explanation of Marketing see Chapter 11.) For any company owner or executive who wants their operation to be more than a source of their own personal compensation, they should understand both sales and marketing as well as how both functions can be applied to the growth of their company. Let's look first at sales.

To understand how to sell a product or service, start by examining the purchasing decision. List all of the factors that most influence a customer's decision to buy and then rank those factors by most to least important. Those factors might include quality, design, performance, utility, simplicity, technological advancement, price, size, weight, delivery time, inventory control, customer training, after sales service, the distance from you to your customer, your company's reputation, and your company's prior relationship with the customer. Once you have a good feel for what causes a customer to chose your product or service over those of your competitors, you can then concentrate on improving those factors which are the most important and present them to your potential customers.

Next, study all possible channels into the markets that use your products or services. Determine how those products or services can be most cost effectively presented to the various markets and sold to the potential customers in those markets. If your customers are limited in number or are all within a relatively small geographic area, direct sales using your own salespeople might be the best approach. For a relatively small company trying to sell

19

products or services to a large number of customers nationwide or in overseas markets, independent sales representatives might be used. Other channels into the markets might include catalog sales, an interactive website, or telephone sales. You should use all of the sales methods that can generate results at a reasonable cost.

By the way, if independent sales representatives are appropriate, they should be chosen with care, well trained by you, and then monitored continuously. (In that regard, also see Chapter 53.) I have a friend who has spent most of his long career consulting only in regard to independent sales representatives. He finds appropriate products and services for reps, and he finds appropriate reps for companies. He has often told me that training sales representatives is as important as finding and engaging the right ones.

Once you've reached an agreement for an independent sales representative to carry your company's products or services, you should have them visit your facility at your expense. Make sure they know your company's key managers, understand how its products are made or its services are provided, and know all of those factors which effect a customers' buying decision. Your sales manager should also make periodic sales calls with each of his or her sales reps. Have those reps devote a day or two to only your products or services with your company's sales manager there to demonstrate the sales techniques he or she uses.

Also, get each of your reps to give you quarterly sales goals and then monitor their progress toward those goals no less than monthly. Those who don't produce should be replaced. In most instances, however, if a sales representative isn't performing, it's more your fault than theirs. Virtually all independent sales reps have more that one product or service to promote. They will concentrate their efforts on those they understand the best or those that will generate the highest return for their efforts. In both instances, it's your responsibility to assure that your reps understand your products as well as the contribution those products can make to the reps earnings. Actively sell to your representatives, and they will sell for you.

Another important element of the sales function is to understand the sales cycle. Is your product or service one that is purchased immediately when needed or one that is sold over an extended period of months? Do your clients inventory your product? Do they use it or resell it, and if they use it, what is the cycle associated with that use? From the first presentation of your product or service until the purchase decision is made, how can you best follow up with the potential customer? A sales program that addresses these questions and is specifically designed for the sales cycle associated with your product or service is the one most likely to succeed.

In addition, know your customer and know who your customer is. If you sell products through retail stores, you might think the store's customers are your primary customers. They aren't; the retail store is. The store must make a buying decision before their customers can buy your product.

If you sell to other companies, determine who within those companies will influence a buying decision and who will ultimately make that decision. Once you've determined that, you can then better target your sales efforts.

My father told me years ago that the two most important elements of selling are to ask for the order and, when you've made the sale, shut up and get out. He was right on both points. Many salespeople do a great job of presenting a product or service but are then reluctant to ask the customer to buy. Make sure you don't have those types in your sales group. As to the second point, I've seen salespeople talk themselves out of a sale after it had already been made. If you've made the sale, there should be nothing else to say other than, "Thanks for the order."

And don't believe the old adage about the mouse trap. If you design and produce a better product or offer a better service, no one will beat a path to your door. With virtually all products and services offered by my many clients over the years, they all had to be sold. They weren't simply bought. Don't just answer your phone; determine how to sell your products or services into a well defined market, and then do it.

21

Chapter 7 - The Peter Principal

I've had several clients over the years who always promoted from within. They wanted to give all of their employees an opportunity to advance within the organization. Unfortunately, some of those employees were either not ready for advancement or not capable of filling a more demanding role. Rather than again promoting them, the question became how to handle their reassignment into a more appropriate position.

Back in 1969, Professor Laurence J. Peter published "The Peter Principal: An Explanation of Occupational Incompetence". The premise for that book was simple but as pertinent today as it was then: "In a hierarchy (such as a company's organization) every employee tends to rise to his or her level of incompetence." In general, if an employee performs his or her job well they will eventually be promoted to a position of greater responsibility and authority. This pattern of promotion continues until the employee reaches a level for which their skills and talents are not suited. At that point, the employee has risen to his or her level of incompetence. They will no longer be promoted to higher levels in the organization because their performance in their current job is poor.

That, however, may not be a reason for dismissal. After all, the employee always performed well in previous positions, has built seniority and loyalty along the way, and, although generally incompetent for their final position, at least makes some contribution. In addition, firing people is always difficult, particularly if their performance in previous positions has been acceptable. Being promoted to their level of incompetence was not their fault but the fault of the person who promoted them.

Peter's Corollary (to the Peter Principal) states that: "In time, every position tends to be occupied by an employee who is incompetent to carry out its duties." Of course, you never find that every employee in a company has risen to their level of incompetence. Most are still on their way up the ladder and are doing their jobs well. Otherwise, the company itself would collapse.

Happily, there are ways to avoid the application of the Peter Principal and Peter's Corollary in most, if not all, business organizations. First, simply recognize the existence of the Peter Principal and don't let it infect your organization. Try not to promote people above their levels of competence. If you make a mistake, and you will, recognize it. Explain it to the person involved, and, hardest of all, move them back into a position in which they can perform well. This may require a reduction in pay, but for the employee, that may be better than having no job at all. In addition, most employees are unhappy in positions beyond their capabilities and might leave if they are not moved backward.

22

Also, don't always relate compensation to organizational positions or responsibilities. It is not unusual that your best salesperson may be more highly compensated than that person's sales manager. That is particularly true if you have a good incentive commission system for your salespeople. If an employee performs exceptionally well but is not suitable for further promotion, recognize that performance with higher compensation even if that salary may be above those of his or her superiors.

When I develop Strategic Plans for my clients, I always include two organization charts in the Plan. The first shows the organization as it functions today; the second shows the organization as it might look two or three years in the future. I show vacant positions in shaded blocks with, of course, many more vacancies on the future than the current chart. Those organization charts help the senior executives not only understand how their company's managers and employees interact but also help them plan promotions, hiring priorities for new positions, and manpower levels and needs related to projected growth.

I also explain, usually with a note on the chart, that vertical positions do not necessarily correlate with levels of responsibility. The positions and connecting lines relate only to definitions of the areas of responsibility and to internal communications. Those organization charts, as well as the entire Strategic Plan, are then shared and discussed with all company managers.

Another method of avoiding the Peter Principal is to compile written job descriptions for every managerial position in your company. This can be a particularly interesting exercise. Start by asking each manager in your company to write their own job description in only two or three paragraphs. Each of those should then be reviewed by the person's immediate supervisor, discussed with the manager who wrote it, and then revised to reflect those discussions.

The revised job descriptions should outline the specific responsibilities of each job and the methods by which performance will be judged. They should also define the position the job will hold within the organization, that is, to whom does that manager report and who reports to him or her. As the job descriptions are drafted and discussed, they should all be reviewed by the person at the top of the chart. If people understand their jobs, their positions within the organization, and their lines of reporting and authority, the entire organization will usually function well.

By the way, entire companies and their owners are also subject to the Peter Principal. I have often found that companies grow until they reach a level that is beyond the ability of the top executives to manage the organization and continue its growth. Those companies either stagnate, decline, or cure the problems impeding their further development. That cure is usually simple. The owner or top executives of the company simply hire additional managers with more talent and experience than they have. After those people are hired, pay them well, give them incentives related to job performance, and let them do their jobs.

Don't let an employee's competence in one position act as an automatic qualification for a promotion. Build an organization of competent people well suited to their positions, and your organization will prosper.

(Also see Chapter 2.)

24

Chapter 8 - Distributing Financial Statements

The majority of my clients over the years believed that their financial statements contain some critical, proprietary information that shouldn't be seen by others, even members of their own management team. They feel those statements must be kept secret from the outside world as well as from their own company's executives.

Are your financial statements really that confidential? If one of your competitors knew your financial results for the past three years, would that give them any competitive advantage? The answer to both of those questions is "no". There are, however, compelling reasons to distribute the monthly financial statements for your company to all of its managers and to your bankers, outside accountants, and independent directors.

The first of those reasons is to align the objectives of all managers with those of the company's owners and its CEO. If you want to maximize the revenues, profits, and enterprise value of any company, you can't do that without the assistance of all of its various management personnel. But how can those people judge the success of their efforts if they can't measure the results? My father told me years ago, "You can't achieve any goal you can't measure."

If you believe a 20% increase in profits during the coming year is realistic, that increase might require some decrease in direct costs as well as lower G&A expenses as a percent of sales. In addition, that 20% profit increase might also require an increase in revenues. For each of those functions, the manager in charge should know well in advance what the goals are. More importantly, however, he or she should be given the rationale for setting the goals, the historical perspective on which the goals are based, and the tools needed to judge their progress toward the goals as the year progresses. Those tools are all based on the financial statements of the company.

If during the mid-part of the year, the goal set for one department doesn't look feasible or perhaps will be exceeded, that change should result in a change not only to that specific performance goal but also to others which might be effected. Again, the principal measure for the initial result and for any appropriate change is financial.

I'm a great believer in incentive bonuses for all managers in virtually any company. If the managers benefit directly from their own efforts, those efforts and their related performance for the company will improve. A bonus, however, will be an incentive for superior performance only if it is based on a specific formula known in advance. Each manager should be given not only

25

the formula but also sufficient financial information to calculate their progress toward achieving the bonus. Passing out annual bonus checks that are an arbitrary portion of unknown profits with no direct relationship to individual performance is not an incentive.

Many of my clients have some fear that their managers shouldn't know how profitable their company is. They believe that knowledge might result in demands for higher salaries or give the managers some information that could be detrimental to the company. It won't.

If the company performs well, its managers who are responsible for that performance should participate in the results, not with higher salaries but with incentive bonuses. If the company does not perform well, it is particularly important that all managers know the deficiencies and understand how they might be corrected. For that, they need the financial statements which they can use to measure their own and the company's performance.

Many of my clients also feel that a company's managers should not know what its owners or top executive are paid. Fine, don't show those payments as a single line item on the financial statements. What other information could be found in your financial statements that might be harmful if disclosed? I don't know of any.

As to competitors, customers, or suppliers possibly seeing your company's financial results because you distribute them to its entire management group, what could they possibly do with that information to harm your company? If its financial performance is better than that of its competitors, can they use that information to improve their results? Probably not. If your customers know that your company is highly profitable, will they demand that you lower your prices? Probably not. And if your suppliers know that your company is highly profitable, won't they be more likely to extend better terms for their products or services? If your company is not profitable, your suppliers might even help you correct the problems.

After all, each of the thousands of publicly owned companies throughout the U.S. publish their detailed financial results each quarter for all to see. It doesn't seem to hurt them.

In regard to distributing your company's monthly financials to its bankers, this timely interim information gives them a better understanding of the company and how it functions. They will more readily respond to a request for additional financing. If performance is low, they can often offer advice that might be helpful. As to your outside accountants, they should review your financial performance not only on a yearly basis but also each month. They should be considered and treated as a part of your management team.

I recently represented the sellers of a company for which the Letter of Intent from the buyers had the following provision: "The Buyer will allow a representative of the Sellers to review the Buyer's financial statements provided that the representative will be prohibited from sharing the details of those financials with the Sellers or the Sellers' employees." Wow! That provision raised immediate and substantial questions as to the ability of the buyer to finance the transaction. It also resulted in protracted discussions as to what the buyer needed to hide and almost resulted in a termination of the entire transaction.

What was that buyer thinking? In addition to placing the transaction in jeopardy, after reading that provision, the sellers knew that their managers would lose their previous access to the financial performance of their departments and their company as a whole. The incentive bonuses that had worked well in the past would no longer be incentives. And the attitude of the buyer toward their own executives and managers was suspect.

Your financial statements are the best measure of your company's performance. That performance should be understood by all members of its management team and used to both control and improve that performance. The financial statements should be easy to understand, distributed widely within fifteen days of each month close, and discussed in regular monthly meetings with all managers.

That won't hurt your company; it will make it stronger. (Also see Chapters 5 and 45.)

27

Chapter 9 - Know What Business You're In

When I was a teenager some many years ago, my father asked me if I knew what business Avon was in. "That's easy," I replied, "They're in the business of selling cosmetics."

"Wrong," he responded, "Avon is in the business of hiring and motivating door-to-door salespeople. As soon as they understood that, their company prospered. What they sell is almost immaterial to their primary business of maintaining an effective door-to-door sales force."

He then asked me if I knew what business Hertz was in. Renting cars? "No," he explained, "Hertz is in three distinct businesses. The first and most profitable is the sale of short term automobile insurance. The second is the creation of used cars. And the third is their automobile rental function." As to the creation of used cars, my father explained that Hertz could purchase automobiles at wholesale, rent them short-term for six months or so, and sell them at a profit to their then depreciated value. Hertz was converting ordinary income into long-term capital gains.

Is Midas Muffler principally in the auto repair business? No, their primary business is selling auto repair franchises to individuals with a high probability of success in that business.

In all of the Strategic Plans that I develop with my clients, I include a section on "Business of the Company". That section is a carefully constructed and detailed examination of each element of the client's business operations. Although most company owners and managers believe they understand the business they're in, that is not as often the case as you might imagine.

For instance, the owners and executives at companies which manufacture products often believe they're in the manufacturing business. Over the past fifty years, many of those companies have been crushed by foreign competitors selling at lower prices. The owners and executives at the companies which succeeded realized that their primary assets were their market penetration and their sales and marketing talent, not their manufacturing operations. They began to purchase the products they sold from less expensive manufacturers and could then compete with either domestic and foreign suppliers in their markets.

Any company that manufacturers a product should continually question whether to purchase a component or item for resale or produce it internally. I call that a "make or buy" decision. If the component or complete product can be purchased less expensively and with the same or higher quality from another source, either domestic or foreign, do it. Profits will not only increase,

28

but the company's market position should improve as its competitors who continue to manufacture their products lose market share to lower priced products, including those sold by your company. (Also see Chapter 59.)

Of all the various functions that contribute to an entire commercial operation, sales are usually the most important. Sales, however, although of paramount importance, are only one element of the business of a company.

Several years ago, I had a client whose company produced lasers for military applications. Their primary business was advanced laser development, design, and application engineering. That company could make ten or twelve of any item they had developed. They realized, however, that they were not good at manufacturing a hundred or a thousand of anything. When their development contracts led to such production work, they licensed their designs to companies in the assembly line production business. The royalties they received from those production contracts far exceeded the returns they might have realized from attempting to build a production capacity for which they had no experience.

I once asked the owner of the largest ready-mix concrete company in Atlanta why he was so successful. He responded that his principal success started when he realized that he was primarily in the trucking business. When he could clearly define the demographics and related costs of his concrete delivery operations, he could locate ready-mix plants that would operate at higher capacities than his competitors. That production cost advantage, coupled with lower delivery costs for shorter routes, allowed him to price his commodity product below his competitors but realize higher margins.

Don't assume that you know what business your company is in. Think about all of the aspects of that business which contribute to its success. List and prioritize each of those elements of the business and then concentrate your efforts on improving those that are the most important to growth and profits. You might be surprised to find that your company is in not one but a variety of businesses. You might also be surprised to learn that the most important of those businesses is not the one you thought best defined your operations or your company.

29

Chapter 10 - Words

I have long felt that all communications and, in particular, business communications should be both clear and concise. In that regard, we should not let either our written or spoken words degenerate into a form of cliché laden jargon. That's relatively easy to do, just eliminate all cute little phrases and instead say what you mean. Here then is a list of words you should strike from your vocabulary:

bottom line / best-of-breed (unless you are talking about a dog show) / mission critical / center of excellence / the BIG picture / keep your eye on the ball / win-win / big time (as in "moving up to the big time") / pushing the envelope / thinking outside the box / best practices / the powers that be / closing the loop / Big Brother (unless you are talking about the book "1984") / functionality (reminds me of the "tornadic activity" the TV newscasters mention) / any work ending in "-wise" such as profitwise, saleswise, marketwise / next level as in "taking it to the next level" / give (you, me, them) a heads-up / at the end of the day (unless, of course, it is the end of the day) / and executive as in "executive summary" (What, the summary isn't for other people? Executives don't have time to read the whole document?)

I have noticed that all apartment buildings, even those built with the cheapest materials in the worst section of town, have a sign in front saying "Luxury Apartments". That is the only way apartments come. In a similar fashion, all financial projections are labeled "conservative". It's rare that I see such projections without the word "conservative" attached somewhere. Most frequently, however, they aren't conservative; they're wildly optimistic. (Also see Chapter 20.)

In the Enron 2000 Annual Report, it said, "We have robust networks of strategic assets...which give us greater flexibility and speed to reliably deliver widespread logistical solutions." Huh? In 2001, Enron filed for bankruptcy. They obviously didn't feel they could tell the truth in their 2000 Annual Report, so instead they used lots of words to say nothing.

Gillette says that their corporate goal is to "build total brand value by innovating to deliver consumer value and customer leaderships faster, better and more completely than our competition." What does that either say or mean? I think they must want to use product innovation to sell more stuff and take market share from their competitors. If that's the case, why don't they just say it in language we can all understand?

Years ago, my wife had an English professor who started each year with a challenge to her class. "I'll give $100", she said, "to any student who can tell me of one instance where the word "use" can't be substituted for "utilize".

30

She never paid. Why be pretentious; use the simple, well understood word "use".

I have a sign on my desk that reads "Eschew Obfuscation". That means avoid the use of long words that are either obtuse, obscure, or unclear.

We would all do well to remember that. When we talk, explain complex concepts to others, and try to make ourselves understood by the hundreds of people with whom we communicate each week, we should use simple, clear language. In that regard, you might have noticed that the Introduction to this book includes the phrase,

I know you believe you understood what you think I said, but
I'm not sure you realize that what you heard is not what I meant.

31

Chapter 11 - Marketing

In Chapter 6, I mentioned that the words "Sales and Marketing" are often used as a single phrase without any idea that the two activities are quite different. They are.

Sales is the presentation of a product or service to a potential buyer and then asking for and getting the order. I might add that getting paid for the order is also a sales function, a part of that effort which is frequently neglected by the members of a sales team.

Marketing, however, is making some potential buyer aware of your product or service, creating demand, and then enticing them to buy.

If the first purpose of marketing is to make a potential customer aware of your product or service, you must understand who those potential customers are and develop cost effective methods of reaching them. Start by defining your customer or customers. Write a short description of each customer type and a typical profile for each. Then list all the ways you might introduce your products or services to those audiences. In addition, list the factors that contribute to a buying decision by each type of customer. Rank those, and then make sure that your marketing addresses the most important of the factors on that list.

Among the choices for marketing, there are thousands of different media that can be used. In the print and other media category, the most prevalent are trade and consumer magazines, newspapers, your own company's product or service brochures, and, of course, your internet website.

In the broadcast media segment, TV and radio are the old giants, but those are divided into hundreds of channels, time slots, and audience targets. Today, broadcast media also includes the internet other than your company's own website. That is the use of banner ads and other internet ad types that are continuing to evolve into ever more target specific methods and presentations.

Other types of marketing media include a wide scope of presentation venues from trade shows which are a particularly effective marketing tool for many products and services, down to the silly idea of hiring a small truck with changing advertising messages on its sides to drive around town as a movable billboard.

Marketing or advertising venues are also becoming ever more fragmented. Broadcast media now increasingly includes messages delivered to cell phones and presented on social media. Product placement marketing includes Pepsi cans appearing in kid's video games. And premium "giveaways" now include small computer flash drives with a company's name and logo on the side.

32

Among this confusing plethora of marketing choices, the problem is determining which might be the most cost effective for your product or service. Much of that determination can be based on simple logic.

During the dot-com frenzy of the late '90's, spending several million dollars to present a thirty second Super Bowl ad for a new, and until then unknown, industrial internet portal with no revenues was just ridiculous. I've read many business plans, particularly for start-up operations, that forecast enormous expenditures for marketing with no indication as to why or how those expenses would result in an increase in either awareness or demand for a product or service.

On the other hand, if you sell an industrial product whose performance or functions are high on the list of factors that control a buying decision, presenting that product and explaining those functions in trade magazines can be particularly effective.

In Chapter 4, I discussed the importance of a company website in today's internet connected world. Such a website is not only an effective method of presenting information on your company and its products and services, it should also be at the top of your list of marketing expenditures.

Although it can be particularly difficult to measure the effect of various marketing methods and expenses, there are simple tools that can be helpful. For trade show attendance, keep a record of the number of sales leads generated at the show, the number of orders that resulted from those leads, and the show cost per order. For any product or service, all potential customers contacting your company for the first time should be asked, "Where did you hear about us?" Then keep a record of the responses.

Marketing expenses can be particularly wasteful or unusually effective. For example, I've often wondered if it is cost effective to put a company name and logo on ball point pens given to various people in contact with the company. I think not. On the other hand, Zep Manufacturing became a leader in the highly competitive markets for industrial sanitation and cleaning chemicals using premium giveaways as a principal marketing tool.

For years, Zep filled its salespeople's cars with literally hundreds of cheap Zep premiums from a set of steak knives in March to Halloween candy in October, all with the Zep logo prominently displayed. The Zep salespeople were always welcome by the members of the maintenance department, and they picked up an order with virtually every visit. It was also relatively easy for Zep to measure the cost benefit ratio for those premiums.

In addition to presenting a product or service, effective marketing should also create demand for the products or services. Go back to your list of factors that control a buying decision. Then for each marketing expense incurred by your company, ask yourself how each one addresses one or more of those factors. If a marketing expense doesn't create demand, it's probably a waste.

33

Does the logo on a ball point pen influence a buying decision? Probably not, but a list of product uses and competitive advantages in a company brochure or appropriate print media certainly does.

Every company should have a marketing budget. How that budget is spent will be one element in determining how successful the company will be. For that reason, the application of each marketing dollar should be a carefully considered, results should be continually measured, and funds should be allocated to the most effective marketing media for the specific product or service being sold.

I read an article some years ago that said, "Marketing is only sales with a college education." That college education, however, results from the experience associated with developing a cost effective marketing campaign. Any such campaign should contribute directly to product or service awareness. That awareness should, in turn, include the factors that control a customer's buying decision. Controlling those buying decisions will then create demand and lead to higher sales, the original purpose of the marketing expenditures.

As with virtually all elements of running a company, effective marketing requires only careful consideration, measuring results, and then making appropriate adjustments.

Chapter 12 - Strategic Plans

I don't believe that anyone should start a trip to a new destination without either a map or some directions as to how to find the place. Yet many company owners and executives operate their business without such a map. They simply operate as if each day was only a repetition of the past. They copy what they did during the previous day with little regard for making changes to accommodate a changing world. That's a prescription for stagnation, mediocre results, and little, if any, growth,.

Instead, I believe the owners and managers of virtually every business should look ahead and plan for the future. That continuing exercise should take the form of a written, five year Strategic Plan. In addition to developing the initial Plan with input from all key managers, the Plan should then be reviewed each year and updated. That annual review would then be used to explore any changes during the past year in the company's markets, operations, organization, or financial condition and also project into the future the effects of those changes on the company.

In a recent Strategic Plan I developed with the managers of a client company, the contents and the rationale for each Plan section included:

- History of the Company - You can't understand where you're going without knowing where you've been.
- Business of the Company - You must clearly understand what business your company is in and how you can modify that business definition over time to adjust to changing conditions. That, by the way, is the subject of Chapter 9.
- Corporate Structure & Ownership - This section is used to explore how the current structure and ownership relates to the future development of the company and how both might change over the coming five years.
- Markets & Customers - This includes profiles for both the markets served by the company and its customers in those markets. Those profiles can then be used to explore appropriate market expansion and the acquisition of new customers.
- Sales Organization, Functions, and Marketing - How you reach your markets and convert sales work into orders is among the most important functions at any company.
- Website Design, Use & Interactive Features - A company without a well designed, interactive website that addresses the information needs of its customers, employees, and suppliers is operating in a world that has passed them by. (Also see Chapters 4 and 40.)
- Competition - You can't compete effectively without knowing who your competitors are.

35

- Growth Opportunities - What can or should you do over the next five years to reach specific revenue and profit goals.
- Personnel & Organization - This section includes an organization chart as the company functions today and another showing how the organization might look in two to three years. All vacancies are shown with shaded blocks. The management team at any company and how that team works together should be among its major assets. (Also see Chapter 29.)
- Accounting, Operating Procedures & Administration - This section explores internal financial controls and operating procedures. You can't control what you can't measure. (Also see Chapters 5, 45, and 46.)
- Facilities & Equipment - Matching fixed assets to revenue growth and planning for future capital expenditures is a particularly important part of cash flow analysis and estimating future cash needs and sources.
- Contingencies & Business Risks - What are those external factors which could dramatically effect your company and its operations over the next five years and over which you have little, if any, control?
- Management Comments - In compiling a Strategic Plan, I always interview all key managers in depth. This section simply extracts some of their comments that would be of interest to the other managers, although I exclude such comments as, "John in accounting is a bone head."
- Historical Financials - These, of course, show the financial results of the past.
- Financial Forecasts - These show the anticipated results by quarter for the next two years and annually for the two following years. Financial Forecasts should be one of the principal maps to the future for any company. (Also see Chapters 19 and 20.)
- Notes to the Financials - These simply explain certain pertinent line items in both the Historical Financials and the Forecasts. The Notes also examine any significant changes over time or any non-recurring expenses.
- Action List - This ending section condenses each action item in the Plan into a bullet list with the page reference for each. This comprehensive Action List is then used to set priorities.

A Strategic Plan as outlined above also results from what I call an "Operations Audit". Most companies in the U.S. have their financial statements either reviewed or audited by an independent CPA each year. They never, however, think of having their operations audited, including interviews with their key managers and an examination of their efficiencies (or lack of efficiencies), business processes, organization, and internal controls. Such an Operations Audit is more important to the future development of a company than its annual financial review.

Planning should be a integral part of every company's development, and that planning should be distilled into a written Strategic Plan that becomes a road map to its future.

36

Chapter 13 - Generational Transfers

Y ou won't live forever. We all know that; we just don't want to admit it. Any company, and in particular any closely held company, should have a succession plan in place long before it might be needed.

Some years ago, I had a client who owned and managed a successful high-tech products company he had founded some twenty years earlier. I frequently told him that no one at his company had the ability to manage its operations other than him. He needed a successor but would not hire one. Within a year of his sudden and unexpected death, that formally profitable, $20 million annual sales company was liquidated. Even worse, the owner's wife had signed personal guarantees for company loans.

If you're the CEO of a company, make sure there is someone within your organization who can take your place quickly and with a minimum of corporate disruption. Then make sure that succession plan is either well understood by others in authority or is written and accessible when needed. In addition, it's always good to examine your organization chart periodically to see what employees have the potential to replace those above them. Succession planning should extend throughout a company's organization.

That planning, by the way, does not have to contemplate a death or disability. At some point, any company's owners may want to retire or even just reduce their workload. In that regard, succession planning is also a vital part of any successful retirement plan. I call that a generational transfer: the transfer of responsibility and authority from an older to a younger generation.

Of course, that transfer can be accomplished without any change in ownership. Often, however, a retiring owner wants to transfer not just his or her management duties but also the ownership of the company to the next generation. That generation might include his or her children or just the company's younger senior managers. Such an ownership and management transfer can be structured as an attractive exit strategy for the retiring owner without selling the company to an unrelated, and usually unknown, party.

On a number of occasions, I have used an interesting method which I developed for ownership transfers between generations. Those can include transfers from either parents to their children, from a current company owner to its younger generation of managers, or to both. To accomplish this ownership transfer, I have the members of the younger generation form a new corporation. That new company ("NewCo") is authorized to issue both common and preferred stock (or, in some cases, a second class of common). The participating managers or buyers then contribute a minimum amount of cash to NewCo in a purchase of 100% of its then outstanding common stock.

37

At that point, NewCo is owned entirely by the participating managers and has their contributed cash as its only asset. NewCo then acquires 100% of the outstanding common stock of the older company in exchange for 100% of the authorized NewCo preferred stock (or second class of common). Although there are significant tax considerations related to the form of the transaction in different circumstances, in general, that stock-for-stock exchange can be structured to be exempt from taxes. It, therefore, accomplishes the ownership transfer without any taxes being imposed on the sellers as of the closing date. NewCo then owns the older company as a subsidiary which can be merged into NewCo or maintained as a separate corporate entity with NewCo acting only as a holding company.

The NewCo preferred stock is redeemable by the company at its stated face value, and that value is calculated to equal the enterprise value of the company as of the original transaction closing date. That redemption feature forever fixes the returns to the older generation at the enterprise value of the company they built on the date it was purchased by NewCo. After the closing date, all future increases in that value accrue to the younger generation who hold the common stock and are responsible for the growth and prosperity of the company.

As the preferred stock is redeemed by the company, the holders of the preferred pay capital gains taxes on the difference between their cost basis in the preferred, which is equal to their cost basis in the company they sold to NewCo, and the redemption price paid to them. In addition, if the preferred stock pays a dividend, that payment to the sellers is similar to interest on a note they might otherwise use as a part of the consideration paid to them for their company. The preferred dividends, however, are also taxed to the sellers at a reduced rate, at least under the tax rules in effect when this was written.

Because preferred stock is a part of the equity accounts of a company, that structure for the sale transaction also eliminates the negative net worth that might be associated with a sale for cash and long term notes. In most instances, for such generational transfer transactions, I also include a provision that assures the holders of the preferred stock that a set percentage of the company's net cash flow will be used to retire the preferred.

In addition, although the preferred stock usually has reduced voting rights which clearly give the holders of the common stock control over their company, I set covenants which allow the older generation to take back control of the company in the event that certain performance criteria are not met. I also usually include a Stockholders' Agreement which establishes the relationships between the various holders of the common stock and between them and the company. (Also see Chapter 23.)

That form of generational transfer can have substantial advantages over either a sale of the company to an unrelated party or its sale to the younger

38

generation using a more conventional cash and purchase money note transaction.

By the way, I am strongly opposed to the use of ESOPs (Employee Stock Ownership Plans) for the transfer of ownership between generations or for any other change in company ownership. Among the reasons why ESOPs are inappropriate, there are two which are of primary importance. First, an ESOP establishes a priority claim on the future capital of a company which would otherwise be available to support its growth. When any employee who is a vested ESOP participant leaves the company for any reason, the company is obligated to repurchase the shares held for that employee in the ESOP trust at the then value of those shares. That is the case even if the employee is fired for cause. This future claim on earned capital cannot be planned and tends to accelerate as time passes.

Also, after a certain employment period, all employees must be ESOP participants. I have often wondered, for example, if it is appropriate for the receptionist in a private, closely held company to also be a stockholder. Usually an employee at that level does not understand common stock ownership in a private company. In addition, that ownership does not act as a performance incentive as it would in the case of stock options or bonuses given to a manager or officer of the company. For me, ESOPs are another bad example of social engineering by politicians using the tax code.

ESOPs aside, any owner or executive in a private, closely held company should not plan for the future development of their company without including its future personnel needs and changes in its organization. In all cases, that should include succession planning and an eventual generational transfer of responsibility and, in many cases, of ownership.

Chapter 14 - Public or Private

During the many years of my corporate financing consulting, it seems that hundreds of company owners have told me that their company would "go public". Many of those were only start-up or development stage operations. In addition to the four that I helped with their public offerings, maybe three or four others actually achieved that goal. There are, however, a number of advantages to becoming a publicly owned company and some distinct disadvantages. As a result, I thought it would be interesting to examine both and to discuss the criteria for a successful IPO or Initial Public Offering.

Let's start with the benefits. First, going public is the ultimate exit strategy simply because public investors will generally pay a higher price for an equity participation in a company than a corporate or financial buyer acquiring the entire business. Of course, that high value can only be realized if there is a true liquid market for the shares, and they can be sold into that market over time without depressing the per share price. In general, however, a business owner will receive the highest value for his or her company (or have the highest market value) if it can qualify for an IPO.

In addition, the proceeds from an IPO, and from subsequent secondary offerings, can be used to support the growth of a company without resorting to additional debt. That method of capital formation can be particularly attractive in an environment of accelerated growth requiring continual contributions to both working capital and the purchase of fixed assets.

Another benefit to having a company's common stock listed on an exchange is the use of authorized but unissued shares as a form of acquisition currency. If a series of acquisitions is a viable growth option, offering the buyer's common stock rather than cash can be particularly attractive for the buyer and often also for the seller. The company's stock can also be used as a non-cash method of bridging a gap between a price the sellers will accept and the cash available to the buyer to support that price.

In addition, the use of common stock as compensation in an acquisition can be accretive. That is, if the target company can be purchased at an earnings per share price lower than the EPS of the buyer in the public markets, the share price for the buyer should increase immediately after the closing. For example, if you acquire a company at an effective price of eight times earnings, but the public investors say your company is worth fifteen times earnings, after the closing, the additional earnings for which you paid eight times will immediately be valued at fifteen.

40

Also, the common stock of a publicly owned company can be more easily used in incentive option plans than that of a private company. Once an incentive stock option for a public company vests, the holder of that option can immediately exercise the option and sell enough shares to pay the option or exercise price. In a private company, however, there is no market into which the shares can be sold as a means of paying the exercise price. That often prevents the exercise of vested options in a private company until the entire company is sold or there is some other liquidating event that allows the option holders to realize the gains which resulted from the success of their company. Although stock options in both public and private companies can be attractive methods of rewarding key employees and giving them added reasons to remain with your company, such option plans are somewhat more effective for public companies with less funding restrictions for the exercise of the options.

As to the disadvantages of being a publicly owned company, I believe they are less in number, and that those few are less severe than most company owners think. The major disadvantage to being publicly owned is the cost associated with the production and distribution of quarterly financial statements, annual audits, and other shareholder reporting requirements. In addition, those compliance costs were increased by the Sarbanes-Oxley regulations of 2001. "Sarbox" requires an annual investigation and certification that internal financial control systems and anti-fraud provisions are adequate.

Although all of the public company compliance costs can certainly be significant, I don't feel they are high enough to eliminate the advantages of being a publicly owned company. Because one of the principal criteria for becoming publicly owned is sufficient company size, the cost of regulatory compliance is most often a minor percentage of the company's sales and profits.

Another disadvantage to public ownership is the addition of a fifth constituency for the company that demands both the time and attention of its executives. For virtually all companies, the four groups of primary importance are their customers, employees, suppliers, and owners. A publicly owned company, however, must add the investment community to that list.

To gain the advantages of being publicly owned, there must also be a liquid market for the company's shares. Establishing that market and assuring that it is active is the responsibility of the company and its principals. They must assure that there are multiple market makers for the company's stock. They must also keep the investment community advised of the company's activities, progress, and, on occasion, its problems. All of this is another demand on the time of the principal executives of the company.

In addition, addressing the needs of the investment community requires periodic presentations for annual stockholders' meetings, discussions with

41

potential institutional investors, and meetings with brokers and stock analysts. If you aren't comfortable in a more public environment, don't have either the time or inclination to sell your company to the members of the investment community, and don't want to answer questions that might come from that new constituency, stay privately owned.

In regard to the "public/private" decision for company owners, I recently prepared the following agenda for a presentation I gave to the family members of a company considering a public offering:

Considerations on Becoming a Publicly Owned Company

Advantages	Disadvantages
• Liquidity for the shareholders	• Regulatory costs
• High stock price	• Sarbanes-Oxley compliance and costs
• Enhanced personal choices or options	• Public disclosure and scrutiny
• Common stock rather than cash and debt as an acquisition currency	• Loss of privacy regarding executive compensation and related party transactions
• Facilitates mergers as both a growth and acquisition option	• The market's concentration on quarterly earnings
• Provides a non-debt source for growth capital through an IPO or secondary offering	• Adding a fifth constituency (customers, suppliers, employees, and owners plus the investment community)
• Can be used to accelerate the Company's growth	• Change in the CEO's duties and responsibilities
• Increased public awareness leading to new opportunities and new customers	• Loss of some flexibility regarding decisions which effect short term profits
• Facilitates incentive stock option plans	• Culture change
• Facilitates generational transfers	• Requirements for annual audits
• Culture change	• Independent Board Members
• Requirements for annual audits	
• Independent Board Members	

42

After considering all of these advantages and disadvantages, if you would like your company to become publicly owned, you should then look carefully at the criteria which relate to a successful public sale of stock and subsequent active or liquid market for your company's shares.

First, in order to realize the benefits of public ownership, your company must be of sufficient size to attract an underwriter for your IPO and then the institutional investors, market makers, and stock analysts that contribute to a liquid market for the shares sold in the IPO. In general, that size should be defined as minimum annual sales of $75 to $100 million.

Also, without a listing on at least the Nasdaq Capital Market (formally the "SmallCap Market") if not the larger National Market, your company will have difficulty establishing liquidity or an active after-market for the purchase and sale of its shares. The minimum initial requirements for a Capital Market listing are Stockholders' Equity of at least $5 million, after-tax profits of more than $750,000, one million shares held by no less than 300 public investors, a minimum share price of $4.00, and three or more market makers.

Even if those listing criteria can be met, your company will find it difficult to address the needs of its new investment constituency if it does not have a realistic plan for future growth of its sales and profits. The rates of that growth must be sufficiently high to contribute to both a relatively high share price and increases in that price over time. Stagnant companies might be good sources of continuing income for their owners but don't usually attract public investors or owners who cannot share in that cash source.

If your company qualifies for public ownership, you should carefully consider the advantages and disadvantages of such ownership. That investigation should include the impact of having public shareholders in your company as well as the impact that ownership might have on you. Many companies clearly qualify for public ownership but should, and do, remain closely held. Others find that the advantages of conducting an IPO and subsequently adding the investment community as a constituency far outweigh the disadvantages.

43

Chapter 15 - Corporate Waste

I know several attorneys who believe that the United States Postal Service has been eliminated and replaced by FedEx. They send even the most mundane items by FedEx at ten times the cost of postage stamps. Make sure such attorneys aren't spending your money on those deliveries.

You work hard to generate your company's profits; don't throw any of those profits away with corporate waste. After all, the elimination of one dollar of waste results in a dollar's increase in profits, and it's often much easier to stop corporate waste than to increase prices or reduce other operating costs.

As you review your monthly financial statements, look for expenses or line items that might be hiding unnecessary costs. In particular, examine the following for corporate waste:

Advertising - Many companies continue to use media advertising that has become either nonproductive or inappropriate. Ask yourself who among your prospective clients will actually see your ads and react to them. I've had too many clients who believed that higher advertising dollars would solve sales problems; they seldom do. Although marketing can be an effective sales aid, it is not usually the solution to anemic revenues. (Also see Chapter 11.)

Your corporate membership in the **Chamber of Commerce** - What does that really give your company other than a small plaque to put on the wall and high salaries for Chamber employees who do little other than solicit more members to pay more fees? The head of the National Chamber has a multimillion dollar annual salary which is paid by the members. Are your company's Chamber dues cost effective? I doubt it.

Cell phones - Do you really need as many as your company has? Which employees need them and which don't? And how might you reduce your mobile phone costs with a review of your total plan and the types of phones you supply to your employees?

Of course, **Travel and Meals** are always areas where waste may occur and be relatively easily reduced.

Penalties should not be a line item on your income statement. If it is, determine what penalties are being paid and why. There should be none.

Although **Bad Debts** are an expense for most businesses, you should calculate their relationship to revenues and their trend over time. It may be impossible to eliminate your bad debt expense but, if it is high, you may have either credit approval or collection problems. Find out which and correct it. Set maximum bad debt goals and see that others in your company understand

44

the costs associated with giving away your products or services for free to customers who can't or won't pay.

Another cost that should be carefully monitored is **Warranty Expense**. If it's high, you have a problem with either quality control or your warranty procedures. I recently had a client devoting just over 2% of revenues to warranty expense, the highest of all that company's G&A Expenses other than salaries. Reducing that single item to less than 0.5% of sales increased profits by over 50%. It also, by the say, resulted in production improvements that increased customer satisfaction.

If your company manufactures a product, you should also develop a method of calculating **Scrap Production** in relation to the quantity of goods manufactured and then examine scrap trends over time. Scrap is material you buy and then throw away. The less you throw away, the higher your production efficiencies and your profits.

Not all companies have the financial strength to take advantage of **Early Payment Discounts**. If you can, do it. Seek suppliers who offer such discounts or ask those who don't if they will. If you can't take the discounts offered, determine what you need to do to change that. After all, a 1% discount for a ten day payment is equivalent to a 36% annual rate of return. Increasing your bank credit line to cover discounted invoices is a quick way of getting that return.

About thirty-five years ago, I managed a brick manufacturing facility in a turn-around effort. Each week, I had a foremen's meeting to discuss operating problems and solutions. Prior to one of those, I spread $10.00 of nickels on the floor. Back then, of course, a nickel had much higher value than today. As the foremen arrived for the meeting, they noticed the nickels and began to pick them up. By the time the meeting started, all the nickels were gone.

That was a great lesson. "Bricks", I explained, "cost about a nickel apiece, but when one falls off a pallet or otherwise ends up in the yard, few if any of the workers pick them up."

"You picked up the nickels," I said, "why don't you pick up the bricks?" As a result of that simple example of corporate waste, our yard was cleaner and our otherwise scrap bricks were turned into money.

Waste is an insidious expense that gets you nothing but erodes profits dollar for dollar. In addition to increasing profits by reducing waste, monitoring every aspect of potential corporate waste is an excellent method of identifying seemingly unrelated problems in a number of different operating functions. Wherever possible, eliminate waste in specific expense categories but also determine ways of monitoring the level or extent of waste and then track those expenses and trends. Costs will go down, and profits will go up.

45

Chapter 16 - Directors

Many, if not most, business owners and executives are missing a great opportunity to get valuable advice for free or nearly for free. During my years of corporate finance consulting, I've found that most closely held companies have their owners as the sole members of their Boards of Directors. That's often a single person. There isn't much you can learn from talking to yourself or to the one or two partners in your company with whom you talk every day.

Instead, consider forming a true Board of Directors for your company with both inside and outside members who can make a contribution to your operations. As to the inside members, consider one or two non-owner executives or a representative of your company's hourly workers. Choose inside Directors who have a broad view of the company's operations and can, therefore, address problems and questions beyond their own department.

In regard to outside Directors, for many business people being asked to serve as a Director is an honor and is a service they will be glad to fulfill. Over the years, I've served on a number of Boards for client companies and recently serve on two for companies that were particularly interesting. I'm glad to devote that time to those companies' development on a quarterly basis. On occasion, I've been granted modest stock options as a method of rewarding me for my contribution as a Director, but most often I've simply served because I wanted to see that company succeed and felt that I might help.

There are a number of business people who can and would serve on your Board and offer advice. Those members can also help you address problems, review expansion plans, and make other contributions to the success of your company. They should, however, be chosen with care and, most difficult of all, replaced if they do not make a contribution or don't attend regular meetings.

For most of the small company Boards on which I've served, we met each quarter but were given monthly financial statements plus a periodic note from the President telling us of any pertinent developments. (Also see Chapter 8.) In addition, the President always prepared an agenda in advance of the Board meetings with specific topics, questions, and problems he or she wanted to discuss. The meetings generally lasted a half day or less with a minimum of wasted time or idle discussion.

In addition, we always treated the meetings as those of a formal Board with votes on motions and minutes kept as a record of our discussions and decisions. In that regard, if or when you ever decide to sell your company, one of the standard due diligence requests is a review of your Board minutes. Few private companies have them, but showing that level of discipline and

Is This Any Way to Run a Company?   H. Lee Rust

organization can be helpful and can also contribute to a smoother transaction and transition.

Among the potential Directors who can usually offer valuable insight, three obvious candidates are an accountant, attorney, and banker. If anyone you might choose from among those three has an existing relationship with your company and, therefore, feel they have a conflict, ask another person in a similar capacity without such a relationship. One of the Boards on which I recently served had an accountant as a member, but she was not a member of the firm that reviewed the company's financial statements.

Other good candidates for a Board position might include someone from your industry who is not a direct competitor to your company, one of your principal suppliers, or any business person who might have experiences which could be valuable (although usually not a customer).

For most companies, I've generally found that five is a good number for the Board members. The odd number prevents vote deadlocks, and five people tend to waste less time than seven. Nine is way too many; three doesn't give you the diversity that can be helpful.

For Board meetings, I always suggest that the company reimburse all Directors for any expenses associated with their attendance. One Board on which I recently served is in Atlanta. Because attending those meetings required a flight from Orlando, to minimize that expense, we usually held two meetings each year which I attended by conference call and two which I attended in person.

If your company can afford it, a modest payment for attendance at each meeting might also be appropriate. The Director's fees that I've received in the past have been either $250 or $500 per meeting, and with one large company, $1,000.

Another good method of rewarding Board members is to give them incentive stock options. Of course, stock options require that the company provide some method of converting the options into a cash return at a future specified date. Options might be particularly attractive if the company plans some other "liquidating event" such as a sale within some specified time period. I am currently working on an expansion plan for a company which the owner would like to sell in about five to six years. Having Directors assist with that planned expansion and then participate in the resulting growth can make the incentive stock options a lucrative form of compensation for the Directors.

Don't neglect an excellent opportunity to learn from others as you lead your company, encounter problems, and work on its growth. Meeting with outside Directors four times each year to discuss your company and its operations is one of the better ways of getting advice that can't be purchased but can be quite valuable.

47

Chapter 17 - Mission Statements

I've heard company Mission Statements referred to as corporate wishful thinking. In that regard, I've never read a Mission Statement that didn't appear self-serving, contrived, and trite. Why have one? What good can it possibly serve?

I saw one recently which said, "Our mission is to achieve the highest level of customer satisfaction with personalized quality customer service to our client companies. Our management team is committed to the fundamental principal: To Provide Quality Service to Our Customers." That Mission Statement is particularly redundant as if saying nothing once isn't enough. It's also poorly drafted and a bad example of quality customer service.

Not long ago, I saw a cartoon that showed two older men sitting in their private club. One was saying to the other, "I equate success with making money hand over fist." Of course, that would not make a good Mission Statement but aren't profits a major part of any company's mission? Without profits, you can't achieve any of the other admirable objectives a company might have.

Another Mission Statement that caused me to wonder said that the company's mission was "to be a premier national company, dedicated to creating the highest levels of value, producing long-term levels of industry-leading profitability and growth." At least profits are mentioned, but would you guess that Mission Statement was for a bank?

One of the dangers of a grandiose Mission Statement is its use as a pejorative statement when the company doesn't meet the high standards of its supposed mission. Several years ago, this Mission Statement was issued by a company that subsequently filed for bankruptcy in a hail of fraud and accounting slight-of-hand, "We adhere to the highest ethical standards of business practice, contributing to the economic growth and social progress of our nation and society, as we conscientiously fulfill our obligations to our customers and staff," with, I might add, an under-funded pension plan, terminated employees, unpaid suppliers, and horrendous stockholder losses.

Should a company have different Mission Statements for its employees, such as, "To operate efficiently and produce high profits so we can afford to pay our employees [read "executives"] more"? And for its customers, such as, "To supply quality products at a low price but high enough to maximize profits"? I don't think either one works.

Here's another good one, "In partnership with our customers, provide most

48

valued, innovative, high quality solutions to enhance asset safety, reliability and service quality, and contribute to our respective returns on investment." What is "asset safety"? Does reliability relate to the safe assets or to some other unmentioned product?

What is the "Mission" of a corporate enterprise? I don't know. I do know that the four constituents of any company are its customers, its suppliers, its employees, and its stockholders. Maximizing or appropriately balancing the benefits to all of those is one of the reasons managing a business well requires exceptional talent, experience, and dedication. Drafting a Mission Statement that addresses the needs of all of those constituents is impossible. Don't even try.

Don't waste your time drafting a Mission Statement, having signs painted, and adding the statement to your corporate stationary or invoices. Instead, just do as good a job as you can do for everyone related to your company and its markets. Don't publish objectives you can't reach or issue statements that say nothing constructive, and certainly don't attempt to make your company known by a cliché-laden, saccharin-sweetened, bromide that you call a Mission Statement but know you can't achieve.

Mission Statements should be against Generally Accepted Accounting Principal (GAAP) rules.

Chapter 18 - Adapt to Change

W hen I was a kid (long ago), the Great Atlantic & Pacific Tea Company, otherwise know as A&P, was by far the largest grocery chain in the U.S. I also remember when Xerox dominated the office copier market, when IBM took the personal computer lead from Apple, and when the U.S. antitrust department talked of splitting General Motors into smaller competing companies because of its dominant market share in auto sales. What happened to these market leaders of the past?

They wouldn't or couldn't change to adapt to a constantly changing marketplace. Grocery stores much smaller than A&P added deli counters, reduced their prices, modernized their store layouts, and expanded their product offerings. As the Xerox' patents expired, overseas manufacturers built less expensive copiers that were better, faster, and more advanced than those offered by Xerox. IBM ceded its personal computer leadership in similar fashion and then ended up selling its entire PC operations to a Chinese competitor. General Motors couldn't match the automotive quality of the Japanese producers quickly enough or match their use of robots and other advanced techniques on their production lines.

In all of those cases, I believe the executives at the companies were too emotionally attached to their product lines, production methods, people, suppliers, customers, or methods of conducting their businesses. I think back to my father's saying repeated in the Introduction to this book, "Do Something, Even If It's Wrong". The message is easy, if you don't do at least something wrong, you're not doing enough.

I've seen way too many companies falter, and have seen some fail because of a simple inability to change. The cure is easy: Don't become too emotionally attached to any aspect of your company. Question everything, particularly those things that reflect the way "we've always done it".

One of the most difficult jobs of any manager is to fire or demote an under-performing employee. When faced with that task, it's too easy to give the person another chance, much easier than telling them to find another job or explaining that they must accept a lesser position. But is that decision to delay right for either the person who might be terminated or the company? In discussing that question, someone might comment, "John has been with us for twenty years, you can't fire or demote him." But you can, and in many cases you should. Length of service does not necessarily translate into optimum performance. In addition, by keeping under-performing employees, you might jeopardize the jobs of many more people at your company. (Also see Chapter 7.)

The ability to change, to adapt, to question, and to act are all more related to performance and personality than to the number of years a person has been with a company. Those qualities are not in any way related to age; a younger employee may find it much more difficult to modify his or her work patterns than someone much older who has experienced, and made, more changes during their career.

Many years ago, my father was a minority participant in two brick manufacturing companies. One used beehive kilns to cure the brick, a process not too dissimilar from the original curing methods used by the ancient Egyptians. The other had converted to a more modern continuous tunnel kiln process. Although the owners of the beehive plant talked for some years about investing in a tunnel kiln, they could never justify to themselves the required expenditure. That old beehive plant was closed and liquidated long ago. The tunnel kiln plant is still in operation and has since been modernized and virtually rebuilt several times over the years.

The way you've always done it might not be the best way to do it today.

If you find it difficult to compete with lower priced goods from overseas sources, phase out your manufacturing operations, buy from the overseas suppliers, and convert your company into a sales and marketing operation. If you question shipping all of those manufacturing jobs overseas, isn't that better than all of your employees losing their jobs in a bankruptcy? (Also see Chapter 59.)

During the 1950's, Howard Johnson's had an opportunity to rival McDonald's in convenience foods. It didn't. In the 1980's, it could have become the Cracker Barrel of the highways. Again, it didn't. Instead, McDonald's offered food cheaper and faster than Howard Johnson's, and Cracker Barrel pioneered a combination down-home cooking and country store concept. Meanwhile, Howard Johnson's let its restaurants deteriorate and finally attracted the slogan "Where the ice cream comes in 28 flavors, and the food comes in one".

A good manager periodically questions every element of his or her business and compares its operations to changing market tastes, procedures, price points, and any other function that might need to be modified, updated, or scrapped. The best managers attempt to forecast market and other changes that might effect their business. Then they either change their operations before the effects are felt or otherwise lead the market. The ones who do that best are generally the leaders in their industries. They also tend to generate the highest levels of profit.

Don't fall in love with the past, with the way your company has always functioned, or with the items in the past that have contributed to its success. They may not continue to be contributors in the future.

51

Chapter 19 - Budgeting

Many companies compile annual budgets for their income and expenses. Then each month they compare their actual results to the budgeted amounts. That works well for the first few months of the year. In November and December, however, the managers are comparing the month's activity to a budget that is a year old. It's as if they assume there had been, or would be, no change in the company or its markets during a full year. Because there are always many changes, that typical, annual, budgeting system becomes increasingly useless as the year progresses.

As a result, I've found it's preferable to budget by quarter, not by month, and to extend the budget for eight quarters into the future. For the current quarter, the budget is divided by three with the actual results substituted for the budgeted amount each month. Rather than have this month-by-month comparison done by the accounting department, it's better to have the numbers added to the budget form by the manager for each department or corporate profit center. That forces the managers to consider the performance of their department each month compared to a budget that is never more than three months old.

The columns for the actual results during the three months of each quarter provide tracking information as the quarter progresses with a monthly measure of how each department is progressing against their budgets for that quarter. When the quarter ends, the person responsible for each of the company's divisions or profit centers then meets with their immediate supervisor to review that quarter's performance. In other than the largest companies, it is good to include in those meetings all of the department heads. In that way, the discussion of one department's performance that might effect, or be effected by, another department is also discussed.

Either during or after these quarterly budget review meetings, each department manager updates their budget for the next seven quarters with the latest information from the quarter just ended, as well as their view of the company's markets and operations at that time. The completed quarter is dropped (other than the year-to-date column) and an eighth is added. In that way, all Company managers are always looking at an income and expense budget based on information that is never more than three months old, are looking forward for eight quarters, and only have to update and meet to discuss the budget every three months.

Forward looking budgets which are updated quarterly can help with production planning, an assessment of equipment and cash needs, an evaluation of sales and marketing efficiencies, pricing issues as markets change, and other elements of company planning. In addition, the managers' work with the budgets can reinforce their understanding of accounting controls, the progress being made by their department and by the company as a whole, and the importance of the entire budgeting and planning process.

When first implementing this quarterly budgeting system, the initial budgets may not be particularly accurate and their preparation may be somewhat time consuming. Over time, however, their accuracy will increase and the time spent compiling the budgets will decrease. During that period, the budgets will also become a more valuable planning tool as the company's managers become familiar with their use and the processes required for their preparation.

The quarterly budget planning meetings would replace the monthly meetings often used to review a company's financial performance. In addition to reducing the number of meetings held by the managers, the quarterly budget review should also be a well structured meeting with a written agenda issued to the managers in advance.

By the way, no department budget form should be on more than a single page. If there are too many line items to fit on a single page, there are too many line items; consolidate some of them. The individual department budgets should also be consolidated into a single quarterly income and expense budget for the entire company. That should also fit on a single page. (Also see Chapter 5.)

In addition, the accounting department should convert all of the department budgets and the consolidated company budget into projected quarterly balance sheets. By also discussing the individual balance sheet items and their relationship to the income and expense budgets, all of the company's managers will not only become familiar with the use of a balance sheet as a control tool but also its relationship to the cash control that can be critical to the company's future.

Budgeting can be a particularly valuable and instructive control tool, but only if the budgets recognize a constantly changing business environment and are updated often enough to take those changes into consideration. A budget that is a year old is an historical curiosity; only one that is updated every three months can be used as an effective part of daily management.

53

Chapter 20 - Financial Projections

In the previous chapter, we talked about budgets; now let's talk about financial projections. Typically, budgets are used as an internal management control tool and are, or should be, updated quarterly. Financial projections, however, are more frequently static estimates (or guesses) as to future performance over a set period of time. Such projections are often used in presentations to various financing sources or as parts of a company's strategic plan for the future.

Over the years, I've not only prepared numerous financial projections for my clients but also reviewed hundreds prepared by others. That has given me an insight into the preparation, validity, and use of such financial views of the future. In that regard, let me mention again the use of the word "conservative".

As outlined in Chapter 10, if someone built an apartment building in the worst section of your town and used the cheapest materials possible, the sign in front of that building would say, "Luxury Apartments". That's because the word "luxury" is virtually always used to describe any apartment building. I've also rarely reviewed projections that were not described as "conservative", even if they were based on little more than the most optimistic guesses. Just don't use that word in relation to any financial projections you might compile. It may not only be wrong but can also adversely effect a reader's reaction to the projections. People who review projections on a regular basis, such as bankers or other financing sources, see that word too often and don't believe it when they do.

In addition, most of the "conservative" projections I've reviewed follow the hockey-stick pattern that shows the past, short-term, flat performance of a company followed by an overly dramatic increase in revenues and profits projected into the future. Many of those hockey-stick projections are based on some exaggerated view of the market for the company's products or services.

I've also seen projections that suggest, "If we can only sell our widgets to 1% of the 300 million people in the U.S., we'll all get rich." But you can't reach all 300 million of those people cost effectively. Don't ever base revenue projections on total market size but on the market that you can actually reach and sell. Then describe how you will reach and sell to that market and show in the projections a realistic cost of doing that.

Also, almost no one projects a loss even if short-term losses are inevitable. When preparing financial projections don't lie to yourself, be realistic as to both the future and what your company can actually accomplish during a set period of time and with the limited resources that may be available.

After you compile the revenue projections, which should always be the first step in financial forecasting, then work on the expenses that will be required to reach those levels of sales.

Some of those will vary directly with the revenue, such as direct material costs. Others will be fixed, such as rent, and will not increase with increasing sales until some future plateau is reached. And others will be semi-variable, that is, they will increase with increasing sales but not in proportion to the percent of revenue increase. Good examples of semi-variable costs are supervisory and administrative salaries, most selling expenses, and business liability insurance.

In preparing projections, it is extremely important that you recognize which expenses fall into each of those three categories and treat them accordingly. Any experienced person reviewing your projections will discount them if, for instance, you show occupancy costs as an ever constant percent of sales. Review each line item in the projections and make sure each changes over time in both a realistic amount and pattern.

For most projections, I start with a detailed forecast of revenues by individual product or service category. I then estimate the number of personnel and related compensation costs that will be needed to generate those revenues, including direct labor and both selling and administrative salaries. To generate that data, I include line item schedules for the personnel in each category by number of people and then convert those into dollars including all payroll taxes and employee benefits.

After completing the revenue and personnel costs for the projections, I forecast the other direct costs and related gross profits levels. Only after that top half of the income statement projection is complete, do I then estimate the selling and administrative expenses.

After all of that work is done and the first draft of the projections is available, I then subject them to the "Lee Rust Reasonableness Check". That is: taken as a whole, are the projected results reasonable and are the individual estimates that make up the projections based on realistic assumptions?

By including a high level of line item detail and supporting many of the line item estimates with descriptive notes, rationale, and assumptions, the financial forecasts will gain a sense of validity. They won't be rejected out of hand as being too optimistic or based on assumptions that are not feasible.

Once the income projections are complete, it's then wise to convert them into balance sheet forecasts. That will force you to consider such factors as the average collection period or the anticipated number of days in your accounts receivable and inventories. Investments in fixed assets necessary to produce the level of projected goods or services will also need to be considered as well as the various categories of liabilities needed to support the increase in assets that will accompany the projected increase in revenues.

55

Finally, convert the balance sheet into a detailed cash flow analysis. That will come as a welcome surprise to anyone reviewing your projections because such cash flows are so rarely included. And again, use the "Reasonableness Check" to verify the overall projected results.

Some time ago I heard that the true purpose of financial forecasts is to make astrology appear acceptable. In the event you are ever called on to generate a set of financial projections for your company, make sure that analogy doesn't apply.

Chapter 21 - Enterprise Value

In my corporate finance practice, I'm frequently asked the question, "How much is my company worth?" That question is particularly difficult to answer, in part because any estimate of corporate values is more art than science. There is no magic formula that will tell you with certainty the enterprise value of your operations (other than a secret one I'll disclose below).

In general, an enterprise or corporate value is definitively set only in a negotiation between an unaffiliated buyer and a willing seller who has no particular compulsion to sell and where both parties have reasonable knowledge of the relevant facts concerning the business. That value would be the price, in cash or cash equivalents, that a buyer would reasonably be expected to pay, and a seller would reasonably be expected to accept, if the business were exposed for sale on the open market for an appropriate period of time.

That, however, is not helpful if you just want an idea of what that willing buyer might pay. Although impossible to answer with certainty, with some exceptions, a good range of values is not hard to calculate. Begin with your last three years' income statements. If sales and profits have been relatively stable, compute the average over that period for your net profits before tax after adding back your depreciation and amortization charges and the annual interest paid on interest bearing loans. If sales and profits have grown substantially over that period, just use the most recent year without an average.

The result of that calculation is your average EBITDA over the three year period or for your last and best year. That's an acronym for Earnings Before Interest, Taxes, Depreciation, and Amortization, or what I call the "nominal cash flow of the business". That is the cash flow that is generated with the non-cash depreciation and amortization charges added back and independent of the amount and extent of the company's financing and its tax status.

Now, multiply your EBITDA by a factor that is usually between 3.5 and 6.5. Deciding on that factor is the hard part. If your company is in a highly competitive industry with plenty of participants and low levels of proprietary content, the multiplier would be on the low side. If your company has less competition and holds patents or has other proprietary elements that tend to reduce competition, the multiplier would be on the high side.

For instance, I've bought metal fabrication shops and construction subcontractors for my clients in transactions with prices of 3.25 to 4.0 times EBITDA less funded or interest bearing debts. For two previous clients, I sold a high tech laser research and development company and purchased a commercial software operation with a 75% market share in a highly specialized business niche. The purchase prices for those specialized businesses with a high proprietary content were calculated using multipliers of between 6.0 and 7.0.

After deciding on that critical multiplier for your business and applying it to your EBITDA, then subtract all of your company's interest bearings debts that would be assumed by a buyer. After all, in buying companies, the assumed debts are as much a part of the purchase price as the debt raised independently to pay the cash portion of the purchase price.

The market or enterprise value of your company should be close to the result of that calculation. Of course, that value will be heavily influenced by more than the competitive nature of your markets and the proprietary elements or intellectual property held by your company. The structure of the transaction will also have an influence on the price. For an all cash purchase, the price will be lower than one for which the seller will provide a significant part of the financing by holding a purchase money note issued by the buyer.

Also, most buyers prefer to purchase assets and assume certain of the recorded liabilities. Such an asset purchase transaction will usually have a higher price than a stock purchase. In the asset transaction, the buyer has the tax advantages of writing up the value of the acquired assets to their fair market value on the closing date and then depreciating them from that higher cost basis. In addition, the asset purchase offers the buyer more protection than a stock purchase against unknown, unrecorded, or other contingent liabilities.

In a stock purchase transaction, the buyer is buying the entire balance sheet of the target company and cannot write up the value of the acquired assets. The buyer can also be subjected to contingent liabilities which accrue to the acquired company which maintains its existence and obligations, both recorded and unknown, after the closing. Of course, the seller can, and should, provide protections against such contingent liabilities. That protection, however, is not as effective as buying the assets from the company, assuming only stated liabilities, and leaving both the company and any such contingent liabilities behind.

The choice of an asset or stock purchase, however, will also have significant tax consequences for the seller and, therefore, have an impact on the seller's after-tax proceeds. In a stock purchase, the seller is taxed at capital gains rates for the difference between the selling price and his or her cost basis in their stock. In an asset purchase, the corporation selling its assets will be taxed on that sale. The subsequent distribution by the company to its owners of the proceeds from its asset sale will then be taxed again to them.

58

Of course, that double taxation is not applicable to a Sub-Chapter S Corporation, Limited Liability Company (LLC), or partnership. All of those corporate entities have "flow-through" tax characteristics with the corporate profits allocated to the company owners and taxed to them as individuals. For an asset sale by such a company, the taxes imposed on the transaction are also taxed only at the individual rather than the corporate level.

Leaving those complications aside, once you have an idea of the value of your company, the question then becomes, "How can I increase that value over time?" One particularly effective method of doing that is to accelerate your growth by acquiring other related companies. In doing that, or in expanding your markets internally, you might also add proprietary elements to your operations that will contribute to an enhanced market value. For instance, a metal working job shop might identify specific products that it could produce and sell at a higher gross margin than competitively bid work for other manufacturers.

But now, for the magic formula which I promised above: that universal multiplier that will give the true value of any company under all circumstances. Although that multiplier is a closely guarded secret, I can include you in the few who know it. The universal multiplier for establishing with absolutely accuracy the enterprise value of any company is "one" times "the purchase price". Works every time.

If you understand the market value of your company and how it might be calculated by a buyer, you can take steps to increase that value over time. Doing that is a principal part of my corporate finance practice and should be an integral part of good company management.

Chapter 22 - Incentive Compensation

I'm a great fan of incentive compensation. In most instances and if properly structured, such incentives can contribute to an increase in a company's revenues and profits. They align its managers' objectives with those of the company's owners and can also be used to prevent those managers from leaving for another job. If the incentives are working well, the related increase in a manager's compensation makes it difficult for another company to match their total salary and bonus. In addition, both incentive compensation and stock options can vest over time. Those vesting provisions would penalize a key employee for leaving your company before the end of the vesting period. That is a form of "Golden Handcuffs" that can also be valuable.

There is, however, a cost to incentive compensation beyond the cash payments to participating managers. No incentive is effective unless it can be easily understood by the person receiving the incentive. In addition, that person must also have the ability to calculate his or her progress toward the incentive or the amount of the incentive earned at any time. That dictates giving each manager the financial information he or she needs to make those calculations. As I've said before, however, you should share all of your company's financial statements with all of those managers who can influence its financial performance. Don't horde the data that your managers can use to identify problems, make corrections, and increase your company's profits. (Also see Chapter 8.)

As to bonuses, in addition to their structure and amount, you must also decide who should participate. In general, I like to extend bonus compensation to all of those employees who can directly influence a company's financial performance. At the highest levels of management, I usually structure bonuses as annual payments. I also base a portion of the bonus on the results of the department or function under the direct supervision and control of the manager plus a portion related to the performance of the company as a whole. That structure not only rewards the manager for his or her individual performance but also gives them an incentive to cooperate with other departments and to be concerned with the entire company's operations. If you want to use vesting as a part of the bonus plan, you can pay the majority of the bonus when earned but reserve a portion for payment at some later date and only, of course, if the manager is still with the company at that time.

For lower level managers, quarterly bonuses might be more appropriate than annual payments. In general, employees at lower levels within a company are best rewarded over shorter periods. A payment within three months can be more effective for a foreman then a payment that won't be made for a full year. For hourly or non-management employees, I've found that bonus payments should usually be made monthly and be based on a single performance objective. For instance, I have a client who gives all hourly employees a monthly bonus based on production levels per man-hour above a threshold level. Another of my clients with a number of retail stores rewards the store personnel for their monthly sales levels again above a specified level.

To make these lower level bonuses effective, the manufacturing company posts the production level each week on a large sign in the shop. Each shop employee can see each week if they are likely to reach the bonus level. The retail sales company includes a calculation of the store's month-to-date sales in each employee's weekly payroll check.

In case you wonder about the cost of such bonus payments, if properly structured, the increase in your company's profits will more than compensate for the bonus expense. Would you rather have 100% of $10.00 or 95% of $12.00. That's not a hard question to answer.

In regard to stock options, those should be reserved only for executives who can clearly understand the long-term benefits of an equity participation in a corporate enterprise. Those executives should be able to understand not only an increase in equity value over an extended period of time but should also think like an owner rather than an employee.

For closely held, private companies, I usually structure stock options such that the executive can exercise the option at any time after its vesting and up to seven to ten years after the original award. I also provide that the executive can then sell the shares back to the company at a formula price. That provides the option holder with the ability to benefit from an increase in value without some other "liquidating event" such as a sale of the entire company.

In addition, I always attach to stock options a vesting period that can extend as long as five years. That would usually be a 20% annual vesting of the options granted to the executive. In the event the executive leaves the company, all non-vested options would be forfeited, and he or she would have a short period in which to exercise all vested options.

That provision might require, for instance, that the option holder exercise the options within sixty days of leaving and then be obligated to resell the shares to the company or to its other shareholders. In the event an option holder is terminated for "cause" as defined in the option agreement, all unexercised options would be canceled and he or she would be required to resell to the company all previously purchased shares at no more than their book value per share.

Stock options reward executives for the long-term performance of their company over a number of years and are particularly effective in extending the executive's planning scope and related performance to include that entire period.

In lieu of stock options, I've also had a number of clients over the years suggest the award of "phantom stock" rather than actual options for the purchase of common stock. In general, I have a strong prejudice against phantom stock as an incentive. One of the principal objectives of a stock option plan is to make a company's executives think like owners. That objective is not only dissipated by the phantom stock concept but also tells the executive that the company owners don't want him or her to join them in the company's ownership. That's the wrong message.

Of course, as soon as you have even the prospect of minority ownership in a closely held company, you should have a Stockholders' Agreement that will control the subsequent disposition of the shares. I'll discuss the provisions of those agreements in the next chapter. Meanwhile, consider how you might use both bonus plans and stock options to increase your company's profits and enterprise value while rewarding the employees who contribute to those improvements.

For a discussion of Equity Capital Accounts as an attractive alternate to stock options, see Chapter 72.

Chapter 23 - Stockholders' Agreements

In the above chapter, we talked about incentive compensation including stock options. In that regard, I also mentioned that any closely held company with more than a single owner should have a Stockholders' Agreement. That is true even for companies owned only by the members of a single family.

You can't predict the future. It is, therefore, important that the owners of a private company decide in advance as to the disposition of the company's common stock in the event of the death, disability, or termination of any stockholder or in the event of an intended sale of shares to any third party. It is also important to address certain corporate governance issues before they become contentious problems with no agreed method of resolution.

In regard to the disposition of the shares after some unforeseen event, I usually provide that first the company and then the other stockholders would have a right to purchase any shares held by an employee stockholder who dies, is permanently disabled, or leaves the company for any reason. That provision requires that the departing stockholder offer their shares to the company or to the other stockholders at a formula price agreed in advance and included in the Stockholders' Agreement. In most instances, I use a simple formula with an EBITDA (Earnings Before Interest, Taxes, Depreciation, and Amortization) multiplier less funded or interest bearing debts. (For that calculation also see Chapter 21.) In the case of termination for cause, I use book value or half of book value.

Stock ownership can act as a particularly effective incentive for the key managers of a company. However, once an employee stockholder leaves a company, his or her relationship with the other stockholders changes, as does his or her objectives or attitude toward that ownership position. It is usually best to give such departing stockholders a method of converting their ownership into a cash return; it is also best to give the company the ability to eliminate that ownership by a now unaffiliated holder.

In the case of non-employee partners in a business, if a partner's shares change hands, the new owner may not have the same objectives for either the business or their ownership as the original partner. Having the "Stockholder from Hell" can be disruptive, a source of continuous disputes, and a problem for both the company and its other owners. It's better to eliminate that possibility by preventing the transfer of the shares to some unknown individual, including the heirs of the original stockholder or a divorced spouse.

In the case of death, shares left to the heirs of a former stockholder can end up in the hands of someone with little knowledge of the business and with a strong incentive to question the salaries paid to the remaining employee

63

stockholders, the lack of dividends, or other company decisions that are not pertinent to either their ownership or to the best options for managing the company. It's better to have an agreement to buy those shares and to use an agreed formula price that is fair and is not subject to dispute.

The Stockholders' Agreement should also give the company and its stockholders an option to purchase shares offered by a holder to any unrelated party. That purchase would be at the same price and under the same terms as that proposed by or offered to the unrelated party.

Equity ownership in a closely held, private company can be a privilege. Unfortunately, it can also be a source of disputes, misunderstandings, and injured relationships. The owners of any private company can use a well structured Stockholders' Agreement to control the ownership of the company's shares and to prevent that ownership from becoming a source of contention. In most instances, a closely held company should remain just that, a corporation owned by a small number of people who, as closely as possible, share short and long term business objectives.

It is also wise to use a Stockholders' Agreement to address a number of important corporate governance issues. In most of the Stockholders' Agreements I've structured, I provide for "super majority votes" that in effect give veto rights to minority owners for certain critical corporate items.

Those super majority voting requirements include both stockholder votes and director actions and usually relate to (a) the removal or hiring of certain officers or directors, (b) any shareholder distributions, (c) any related party transactions, (d) the sale by the company or of any additional shares or any loan convertible into shares, (e) the sale of any significant assets, (f) stock option awards, (g) amendments to the Articles or By-Laws, (h) the purchase of any assets above a threshold amount, (i) borrowing money or approving any such obligation above a threshold amount, (j) the approval of any contract with a value exceeding a threshold amount, or (k) the repurchase by the company of any of its shares.

In addition, I often provide an agreement that the stockholders will vote their shares to maintain certain members of their group as directors. I also add that the directors will cast their votes to maintain certain individuals as officers of the company with specific titles and responsibilities. Those positions usually remain unchanged as long as the individual remains a stockholder and is willing and capable of fulfilling the duties of the position.

A well structured Stockholders' Agreement can prevent a closely held company from dissolving in an atmosphere of distrust, conflicting objectives, and continuous disputes. In his 1915 poem "Mending Wall", Robert Frost said, "Good fences make good neighbors." In similar fashion, a Stockholders' Agreement can make good partners.

Chapter 24 - Articles & By-Laws

This is one of those chapters my wife says reads like eating dry Grapenuts, but some subjects are inherently drier than others. That doesn't mean they're not important. For example...

How often do you think about your company's Articles of Incorporation and By-Laws? Those documents are probably like your little finger: not something that is of significant concern on a regular basis. They should, however, be reviewed every couple of years and updated to match your company's plans and objectives. If you ever expect to consider growth through acquisitions or mergers or an incentive stock option plan or raising equity capital to support accelerated growth, you should make sure the number of shares authorized in the corporate Articles is sufficient to undertake those objectives.

Also, in your Articles of Incorporation, is the Registered Agent some attorney who formed the company years ago and is no longer involved or are the original owners listed but with addresses long out of date or with an earlier partner who is no long involved? The Articles of Incorporation for a company are usually only two or three pages long, but those few pages should reflect the current status, organization, and objectives of your company.

Of even more importance, the By-Laws of most companies were written at the time of the company's original incorporation by an attorney who used a standard form for a new entity. It's all "boiler plate". That might have been fine when the company had minimal operations but may not be suitable for the current conditions.

In particular, are the stockholder voting provisions consistent, for instance, with having a minority partner? Are the number of Directors and their qualifications appropriate? Are physical stock certificates required in a time when digital storage has eliminated the need for such formal, engraved paper?

I recently reviewed the Articles and By-Laws for one of my client companies. In the By-Laws, the notice provisions still assumed that the U.S. mail and telegrams were the only delivery service. There were no proxy voting provisions and no stated method of adding any additional classes of stock or equity securities. Of more importance, there was no mention of a Stockholders' Agreement, something every company with more than a single shareholder should have. (See Chapter 23 above.)

In addition, "cause" for the removal of a Director or executive included only "conviction" of a felony when it should have been based on indictment. After all, the time difference between those two can be years. Also, the

"Officers" section did not provide for a Chief Executive Officer even though the company had long had a principal owner in that position. I suggested numerous changes to those By-Laws, some significant and some only minor wording, but they were on every page.

While you're considering such changes, look at the provisions for stockholders' and directors' meetings. Most small, closely held companies never hold those meetings but should. If you ever plan to sell your company or take it public or merge with another entity, one of the items on the due diligence checklist will be copies of your board and stockholder meeting minutes. You should have them. (Also see Chapter 16.)

In regard to your company's corporate organization, virtually every closely held company which qualifies should make a Sub-Chapter S tax election. Under that "flow-through" method of taxing the corporate income at the owners' level, there are substantial tax and corporate options that are not available to a regular "C" corporation. Among those, the most important are an enhanced ability to reorganize the ownership of the company's assets with reduced tax implications and the ability to sell the company in an asset purchase transaction without double taxation. (Also see Chapter 21.)

Under the Sub-Chapter S form of corporate taxation, if the company sells its assets, the capital gains associated with that sale flow through to the company's owners and are taxed only at their level. In the case of an asset sale by a C corporation, the corporate entity is taxed on the sale proceeds. Those proceeds, however, are taxed again when they are distributed to the company owners as dividends. Because of the contingent liabilities that can be associated with the acquisition of a company in a stock purchase, virtually all buyers prefer an asset purchase and will usually assign a higher value to the company in such an asset purchase.

A more recent form of corporate organization available in most states is a Limited Liability Company (LLC). Like a Sub-Chapter S corporation, the earnings for an LLC flow through to its owners. The LLC, however, offers somewhat more flexibility than a Sub-Chapter S corporate structure.

In particular, an LLC can have a corporate owner while a Sub-Chapter S corporation cannot. The LLC can also have several different classes of stock while the Sub-S Corporation can have only one. Those differences might not seem important until a private equity or venture capital firm turns up as a source of growth capital or when a second class of stock could be used in a generational transfer or management leveraged buyout (MBO).

Another important element of corporate organization for closely held companies is the ownership of real estate. I always suggest that operating companies not own real property. Any land and buildings used by a company should be owned by an unrelated party or by its stockholders and leased back to the company. Even in Florida where sales taxes are imposed on leases, I suggest that form of split real property ownership.

At some point, many companies are sold as a means of converting their ownership into a cash return. Because enterprise values are most often based on earnings, any real property owned by the company may not contribute to its purchase price. However, if the company and the real property are sold in separate transactions, even to the same buyer, the price paid for the company will usually be based on its earnings while the price paid for the real property will be based on appraised values. The sum of those is almost always greater than the sales price of the company with its physical facilities simply carried as another asset on its balance sheet.

In the day-to-day environment of producing and selling good or services, corporate organization might not seem particularly important. It becomes important, however, when any change of ownership or corporate status is considered. At that point, it is usually too late to make changes that could enhance the value of the company or otherwise facilitate a capital formation opportunity. Review your company's Articles, By-Laws, and related corporate organization periodically and keep them current with both your present and future plans and objectives.

Chapter 25 - Step Function Growth

Too often I see company budgets or financial projections that show a smooth increase in sales and related expenses. Corporate growth, however, is never linear. Instead, the growth in expenses follows a step function as capacity is added to match increasing sales.

Think of a simple manufacturing facility operating at less than capacity. As sales increase, the cost of manufacture as a percent of those sales should decrease. The same number of employees and equipment produces more goods for sale. That relationship holds until the facility is operating at full capacity. At that point, however, any increase in sales will require an investment in more people, more machinery, and higher utility expenses to run the machines. As those expenses step up, the manufacturing cost as a percent of sales also increases, and gross profits go down.

In addition, at some point more people will be needed in administration, and those expenses will also step up. With the new capacity in place, however, the continued growth in sales can once again result in a decrease in costs as a percent of those sales. That shows step function growth as it actually occurs.

As you might imagine, the step function related to the growth of expenses is more pronounced for a small company than for a larger one. If you have only two people in manufacturing, adding a third to increase capacity increases direct labor cost by 33.3%. If you have twenty people, adding another increases labor cost by only 4.8%. Big difference.

When planning your company's budgets, compiling projections, or simply thinking about the effects of a growth in sales, don't forget the step function and the relationship between capacity and expense. The sales growth might be a smooth increase or close to linear; the related expenses won't be.

Although it seldom happens, in my long career, I've even seen profitable companies grow into bankruptcy. Once full capacity was reached, the cost of making the next step up to support a higher level of sales exceeded the company's ability to finance the increase in costs. The result was a lack of cash and related working capital that then caused problems with suppliers and eventually lead to losses that could not be sustained.

In earlier chapters (principally in Chapters 19 and 20), I've talked about budgets and financial projections. Those are particularly helpful planning tools but to be helpful they must be realistic. As you plan for growth, think about capacity and output related to your employees, equipment, and facility. When compiling budgets or projections, it's always best to start with sales. Then analyze the number of employees needed to generate those sales in

68

production, in administration, and in your sales department. By adjusting the number of employees in relation to the level of sales and then converting the number of employees into the cost of employing them, you'll see the step function in practice. Do the same for equipment and facility needs and then for other expenses. The results will be a realistic financial forecast that doesn't anticipate a consistent relationship between the levels of sales and expenses.

In business school, corporate expenses are often divided into three major categories: Fixed, Semi-Variable, and Variable. Without embarking on a B-school lecture, fixed costs don't vary with sales until full capacity is reached. Variable expenses do track sales, such as materials purchased for production. And semi-variable costs lie between the other two. As you might imagine, the fixed costs show the greatest step function effect; variable costs show almost none, and semi-variable costs step up at certain sales levels but at a lower percentage than the increase in sales. For planning purposes, it's helpful to understand which of your corporate expenses are in each of those three categories.

Why does the step function matter? Because planning for the future matters, and that planning must be based on a realistic assessment of revenues, costs, and the ability to generate profits as both the revenues and costs change.

69

Chapter 26 - Pricing

Years ago, my business economics professor asked our class how we would set the sales price for a new product. We immediately started discussing a calculation based on the cost of manufacture plus a reasonable gross profit.

"Wrong", the professor interrupted, "first do a market study to determine the maximum price you can charge and still sell appropriate quantities of the product. Then calculate the cost of manufacture only to determine if production of the product is attractive."

Setting sales prices is an art, not a science, and is based less on product or service cost than you might imagine. Markets do, and should, determine prices. Therefore, market analysis is an extremely important part of any pricing decision.

In general, product or service prices should be examined and adjusted on a regular basis depending upon the volatility of the market. Of course, for a job shop bidding individual production projects, prices are set with each bid and the competitive price environment is known with every win or loss. In a commodity market, such as the production of landscape mulch or windshield washer fluids, market prices should be analyzed every few months as well as seasonally when demand peaks. For a proprietary branded product such as scuba diving equipment, prices might be set once or twice a year. By the way, each of those different product examples is produced by a former client of mine.

In setting prices, the tendency is usually to set them too low rather than too high. There is too often a fear of losing market share, suffering a sales decline, or not winning the project award. Those fears depress prices, often well below what the market (or customer) would accept. Continual analysis is required. Raise prices and quickly judge any effect on sales. If a product is not selling at the levels you believe are feasible, lower prices and see if revenues increase. At higher levels of production, costs might even decrease to more than make up for the lower prices.

All of this analysis should be based on a combination of financial and market data that must be current. As I've said frequently, financial statements that are generated more than fifteen days after the close of the previous month are historical curiosities, not control tools. Statements that don't include appropriate profit center accounting for each product line or company division are also useless as pricing guides.

70

In addition, beware of excessive pricing pressure from customers, (See Chapter 1), and watch for competitors who continually depress prices. If prices get too low, either let them have that market segment or maintain a higher price with lower sales only to customers who value quality and service more than the lowest price.

As an integral part of your pricing strategy, train your salespeople not to sell on the basis of price. In conjunction with your sales group, list in the order of priority all of the factors which might control a buying decision by your customers. You may be surprised how low pricing is on that list. Then use that list to convince your salespeople that salesmanship is not offering the lowest price but is, for instance, convincing your customers that their total cost of use might be lower for a higher quality product than for one with a lower price. (Also see Chapter 6.)

In general, sales managers should not set prices without some oversight. In addition, incentives for individuals with some control over prices should rarely, if ever, be based on the level of sales. Only in the case of sales commissions where the salesperson has no control over prices should the commissions be a percent of revenues. Otherwise, sales incentives should be based on gross profits which go up if the salespeople can sell at a higher price.

With most, if not all, of your pricing decisions, attempt to be the price leader rather than a follower. Years ago, my father ran an engineering/construction firm. One of its divisions built large industrial chimneys. That division, however, was a chronic loser. Although the decision was finally made to close the division, my father said that they should not simply exit the business. Chimneys, he explained, are connected to the factories that the company also designed and built, and my father didn't want to alienate those clients. Instead, he suggested that they just bid the chimneys at high prices. They would not be the successful bidder, and the business would wind down with no ill effects. Five years later, the chimney division was one of the most profitable at the company. They became the price leader, and their competitors followed.

In regard to your pricing decisions, you should also periodically test various pricing levels. Either raise or lower prices for specific products or services more than you normally would and measure the revenue and gross profit results. You might be pleasantly surprised. If not, you can always return to the earlier price points.

And with all pricing strategies, remember that markets are never static. Their extent and rate of change should be reflected in your pricing decisions. Base those on market factors, features other than price, and periodically test your pricing against your competitors The art of pricing is a significant part of the art of business. Do it well and your company will prosper.

71

Chapter 27 - Hiring Procedures

Not long ago, I saw a cartoon which showed two men on either side of a desk. One, who had grabbed the other by the tie and drug him half-way across the desk, was saying, "You advertised for an aggressive salesman?"

Hiring excellent people is one of the more difficult jobs faced by any business person. The success or failure of your company will be largely defined by the talent and dedication of its managers and other employees. As important as the hiring task is, however, I have never found a method of determining with much accuracy whether a person can and will perform well without giving them the position and measuring their performance. Even with that limitation, however, there is much you can do to improve your odds during the hiring process.

Today, finding qualified applicants is easier than it's ever been. In addition to the conventional sources of personal recommendations, employment agencies, trade press advertising, and simply advising various market participants of your needs, the internet has become a particularly effective source for locating job candidates. For one of my clients, I recently posted a position on Monster.com for a comptroller. Within a few days, I had received almost two hundred resumes. From that group, I interviewed ten by phone. My client and I then interviewed three candidates in person and hired one of those three.

Of course, one of the problems with that process is reviewing two hundred resumes, not a pleasant task. It's possible, however, to condense the work by establishing a few specific criteria that you judge to be prerequisites to success in the job. Then go through the resumes quickly looking only for those criteria and eliminating the people who don't qualify. Once you have reduced the stack to a manageable number, read each one to decide whether you should talk with the candidate by phone and, for the ones who also pass that test, eventually hold personal interviews.

In regard to such interviews, I have developed, over the years, a generic list of questions that I now always use in the interview process. In each case, I add a few questions to the list which relate specifically to the job being filled and to the industry or market participation by my client's company.

During the job interview, I then take notes related to each question so I won't confuse the candidates when reviewing all of the interviews and helping my client make a selection. I'll include a copy of that list on the next page.

For relatively high level managers, another method of finding qualified candidates and shortening the hiring process is to turn the task over to an executive recruiting firm. There are hundreds of those from the five or six large, major, international recruiters to individuals working out of a home office on a regional or individual city basis. In addition, some recruiters specialize in specific industries. For instance, on several occasions, I've had good results using Robert Half International to find accounting personnel for my clients at the CFO or comptroller's level. That recruiting firm has local offices in most large U.S. cities and works extensively in the areas of accounting and finance.

As with any service, however, executive recruiters can be effective or simply a waste of time depending upon the talent of the individual recruiter. In the case of the most effective, they attempt to locate job candidates who are not looking for a job and would not respond to an internet posting or help wanted ad. They do this by calling industry participants in appropriate positions and asking if they or one of their associates might be interested in moving to a new company. That process, of course, has earned those recruiters the well known nickname as "headhunters".

In addition to finding qualified candidates, executive recruiters should also conduct the initial interviews and, if they are good at their jobs, present you with only three or four well qualified candidates. Although relatively expensive, that process can save time by delegating to the recruiter all of the work up to your initial interview with the final two or three candidates.

As their name implies, executive recruiters are generally suitable only for relatively high level positions. They are expensive, generally charging up to 30% of the annual salary for anyone you hire through them. That expense is cost effective only when you are recruiting for a manager's level or above.

Job Interview Questions

1. Why do you want to change jobs or why did you leave your last job?
2. What do you identify as your most significant accomplishment in your last job?
3. How many hours do you normally work per week?
4. What did you like and dislike about your last job?
5. How did you get along with your superiors and subordinates?
6. Can you be demanding of your subordinates?
7. How would you evaluate the company you were with last?
8. What were its competitive strengths and weaknesses?
9. What best qualifies you for the available position?
10. What salary do you expect to receive?

73

11. What was your salary in your last job?
12. How long will it take you to start making a significant contribution?
13. How do you feel about our company: its size, products, and competitive position?
14. What interests you most about the available position?
15. What control or financial data would you want and why?
16. How conversant are you with reading financial statements and their use for operations control?
17. How would you establish your primary inside and outside lines of communication?
18. What would you like to tell us about yourself?
19. What are your greatest strengths?
20. Greatest weaknesses?
21. What is your job potential?
22. What are your career goals?
23. Where do you want to be in five years?
24. What is your credit standing?
25. How aggressive are you?
26. What motivates you to work?
27. Is money a strong incentive for you?
28. Do you prefer line or staff work?
29. What do you look for when hiring people?
30. Have you ever fired anyone?
31. Will you sign a noncompete agreement?
32. Do you expect an employment contract?
33. Why should we hire you?
34. Do you want the job?

Once you've found and agreed to employment terms with the final candidate, you should then have a background check conducted. There is much you can't determine in an interview that a background check might disclose. In addition, in today's litigious atmosphere, if you don't have a background check on management level employees, you're exposed to litigation in the event you've hired a convicted felon or other unsavory character. Worse, you don't want to hire a CFO, for instance, who has a record of embezzlement. I've seen it happen.

74

There are a number of national firms that offer background checks. I have often used a small company in Sarasota, Florida that offers two day service at reasonable prices. You only need to tell the job candidate that you intend to have a background check performed and ask for their social security number. Only once have I had an applicant question the advisability of doing that. When that happened, that alone was an adequate warning sign. As a result, my client and I went to the next candidate on our list.

After you've found the right person for the job, make sure they agree with you as to the parameters for the job, the early stage problems that need attention, and what you expect from them. (Also see Chapter 2.) Then, you should measure their performance, particularly during their first few months on the job. Confirm that you have found the right person and be sure you have given them the responsibility and authority they need to succeed. Hiring good people is time consuming, difficult, and not usually much fun. Having the right people in the right positions, however, can make the difference between success and failure or between excellent and mediocre results.

Chapter 28 - Nepotism

A mong my collection of business cartoons, I have one which shows two men outside an office door. One is pointing to his watch and saying to the other, "Just because you're my son doesn't mean you get any special treatment around here - even vice-presidents are supposed to be here when the little hand is on the 9 and the big hand is on the 12."

Because my father was the second generation in a family owned business, I have ambivalent feeling about nepotism. In my years of work with small and medium sized companies, I've structured several acquisitions in which the members of a younger generation bought a company from their parents. I've also seen the sons and daughters of company founders both succeed and fail. In both cases, nepotism gave them the job, but their success or failure then depended only upon their own management ability.

In general, I feel that hiring family and friends is not a good idea, not because those people lack the necessary qualifications but because judging their performance is more difficult than with unrelated parties. In addition, if their performance is marginal or worse, reassigning or dismissing them can be extraordinarily difficult and usually presents problems not associated with such decisions for an unrelated person.

That notwithstanding, if a family member wants an opportunity at their family's company and is well suited to the job, there should be no reason not to give them the position. The difficulty is having them understand that the job and their family relationships will be kept separate and to then actually do that.

I've worked with a number of company owners where the sons and daughters were groomed to take over the operations. In the generational transfers that were the most successful, those sons and daughters wanted the responsibility and the ownership positions. They conformed their educational background to the needs of the company and then worked for a significant number of years in a variety of positions within the company they would eventually own and manage.

In the unsuccessful examples of nepotism, the younger generation either (1) didn't have a passion for the business, (2) were not suited to the job by either education, experience, or temperament, or (3) were given management positions and high levels of compensation at way too early an age.

I recently had a client in the contracting business. The founder of that company had a policy of giving significant bonuses to its managers and then allowing them to apply a part of those bonuses to buying an equity position in the company. Over time, those managers became the principal owners of the company. They built it into one of the largest participants in its market area. Those managers, however, became managers before becoming owners, paid for their ownership at near market value, and understood both the long-term value and responsibility of their ownership. That company, by the way, had an absolute prohibition against hiring family members. That policy removed the temptation to create a job for a relative or to judge a relative's performance with criteria different from any other employee. (Also see Chapter 23.)

I also had a client company with eight family members in various positions. It was highly successful and dominated its specialty equipment markets. In addition, it was managed as a family affair. All family members met each quarter to discuss any company issues that involved either the family or the development of the company. Every family member was expected to perform the jobs to which they had been assigned, and that performance was judged more harshly than for non-family members. And of particular importance, one member of the second generation was the President and Chief Executive Officer, was well suited to that position, and was understood to be the boss. All of the family members knew the rules, and it all worked well.

In another instance, however, after the death of a founder at one of my client companies, his son was forced into a management role for which he was not suited. Three years later, the company filed for bankruptcy protection and was eventually liquidated.

I've also counseled the sons and daughters in family companies to prepare themselves for eventual ownership and executive positions. In one instance, the son went back to school with night classes to get his Master of Business Administration degree. That additional education not only contributed to his success in the eventual CEO role but also made him understand the sacrifices needed to take that position.

I've often heard that the first generation forms a family business and works to get it established. The second generation builds the company to significant size, and the third generation wrecks it. Of course, generalizations are never accurate.

In any company, finding, hiring, and motivating good people is one of the most difficult but most important tasks for its owners and managers. (Again, see Chapter 2 as well as 27.) If a family member or friend is well qualified for an available position and wants it, why not give them the opportunity? However, if the job is being created for that person simply because they are related, if they are not qualified by education and experience for the job, or if they don't want the position more than any other they might find, hiring them will probably be a mistake.

In all cases, the difficulty is in judging the qualifications of a family member or friend for a job as if they were not related, assessing their

77

performance after they have the job, and making any changes that might be advisable based on that assessment. In the hiring process, it's a good idea to have any friends or family candidates apply for the job along with unrelated candidates. Then follow the same procedure you would as if no family or friends had applied. Chose the best person for the job. If that turns out to be a family member or friend, make sure they understand that their performance will be judged as if they were unrelated; then do that.

If those criteria can't be met, if you can't separate business from personal decisions, hiring family and friends is probably a bad idea.

In case you wonder what happened in my family's business, my father died, his brother sold the company while I was still in training, and I eventually moved on to other pursuits. As it turned out, I love what I do now which has no relationship at all to the family business. I'm not as wealthy as I might have been, but I'm a lot happier following my own direction in corporate finance than working in a family environment.

Chapter 29 - Organization Charts

If you don't have an organization chart for your company or for your individual department within the company, you should. In fact, you should have two, one showing the way the organization functions today and another showing its lines of authority and responsibility as they might look a year or two from now.

You don't need some fancy computer program to draw those charts. When I'm compiling organization charts for my clients, I just use an Excel spreadsheet to draw the blocks for each position and the lines between the blocks. I also shade or color all of those blocks which represent positions that are vacant. Those charts, particularly the future projection, can then be used for manpower planning, setting hiring priorities, and budgeting for employee compensation.

For all organization charts, I also add a legend saying, "Note: Vertical positions on the chart do not indicate levels of responsibility." Many people think that the higher you are on the chart, the higher your is position within the company. While virtually all organization charts start with the Board of Directors or President at the top, farther down on the chart, convenience and the ability to draw the chart with reasonable dimensions might dictate different vertical placement for positions with similar responsibilities. In addition, a lower level employee in one department might be shown higher on the chart that a more responsible position lower on the chart but in another department with more people. The important element is not vertical position but the accuracy of both the reporting lines and the relationships between positions.

Once your current and projected organization charts are complete, copies should be given to all management level employees with a request for comments. You might be surprised how may of your company's managers don't share your understanding as to how the organization functions. The charts are an effective method of uncovering such misconceptions and misunderstandings. All employees should understand the reporting lines and relationships shown on the organization charts. More importantly, they should also agree with you and among themselves as to how the organization functions.

In regard to the projected organization chart, it should also show both you and other members of your management team how they might advance within the organization over time. That alone can be an incentive to work toward a position of greater responsibility.

79

When developing an organization chart, I try to avoid dotted lines. In general, all departments and all levels are expected to cooperate with the others. You don't need a plethora of dotted lines between departments to show those less formal relationships.

I also don't use round charts or other unconventional methods of describing organizational relationships. Keep the chart in conventional format, simple, and easy to understand.

You should also avoid horizontal organizations. If your chart shows a long horizontal line just beneath the Chief Executive Officer or any other manager, he or she isn't delegating enough responsibility and authority to others in the organization. In general, no person in a corporate environment should have more than six or eight people reporting directly to them. If they do, they're probably overloaded.

Organization charts can also be used to identify other areas of particular strength, weakness, or inappropriate relationships between departments. There may, for instance, be individuals or managers with too many job titles. I recently developed an organization chart for a client company that showed the Sales Manager as also having responsibilities and titles for Marketing, International Sales, IT Manager, Graphics Manager, Customer Service Assistant Manager, and Assistant to the General Manager. Just listing the titles showed that drastic changes needed to be made. The projected organization chart then showed how those changes would be made and how the Sales Manager's job would be divided among additional people.

Reviewing your current and projected organization charts is a convenient way to think about the various managerial positions in your company, which individuals are performing well, and who might do better. Rather than terminate an under-performer, study where they are on the chart. Consider what changes could be made in the reporting lines to better support that individual, give them additional training, or define a job for which they might be better qualified or suited.

Then update your organization charts each time a change is made in your management group. You should periodically use your organization charts to examine, question, and refine how your company functions and how its managers and other employees interact. In that regard, current and projected organization charts are particularly effective in helping you maintain or improve the efficiency within your organization. Higher efficiencies, better communications within and between departments, and an understanding of reporting lines and responsibilities will lead to higher profits.

By the way, both current and projected organization charts should always be included in Strategic Plans and are an important element in the planning process.

80

Chapter 30 - Acquisitions

A mong the growth options for your company, there are two major categories: Internal and External. Internal growth is simply selling more of your products or services by increasing your market share within your current market areas. External growth is the acquisition of another company or a merger, joint venture, or partnership with another participant in your markets.

I have long wondered why so few companies consider acquisitions as a growth strategy. Why spend what could be years attempting to increase your company's sales by 50% or more when you might accomplish the same goal with a single acquisition that could be closed in four to six months?

In considering acquisitions as a method of accelerating your company's growth, let's consider the basics. For either a single acquisition or a continuous acquisition program, there are only three absolutely required elements:

1. **There must be something to buy.** That might sound ridiculous, but if you want to move into the Chicago market and that city has only two competitors in your industry, if they both say "no", there's nothing to buy. If there are 35 candidates, as there were for a search I did in Atlanta, your chances of completing a purchase are excellent.

The easiest acquisitions are done in a fragmented industry with a large number of relatively small participants. The exception to that rule is the purchase of a single competitor or target company that you know to be available. That definitely gives you something to buy.

2. **You must be able to manage what you buy.** Operating a remote facility or several subsidiaries is quite different from the management of a single location. For a successful acquisition, your company should have sufficient management depth and talent to not only assimilate the acquisition but also assure its continued profitability as a part of your operation. In addition to people, this management requirement also relates to the financial and reporting systems necessary to monitor, control, and react to changing conditions at multiple facilities.

This does not mean, however, that all of the desired people and systems must be in place prior to closing an acquisition. I've structured many acquisitions where part of the needed management talent was in the acquired operation rather than the parent. I've also developed reporting and control systems to fit an acquisition as a part of its transition plan rather than having those systems already in place.

3. **Finally, you must be able to pay for what you buy.** The price, payment terms, and subsequent cash flow of the acquisition will have an enormous impact on how your company might finance its purchase.

81

You will, for instance, need resources sufficient to not only close the transaction but to also make necessary working capital and other contributions to the acquired company's operations and future growth. In determining how much you can afford to pay, and therefore an appropriate target size, you should carefully assess your company's financial strength and your appetite for risk. This requires a thorough evaluation of the historical financial results of the target company and the development of pro forma statements showing those past results with adjustments as if the company had been owned by a corporate parent during those periods.

Based on those historical and pro forma financials, you can then produce projections factoring in the acquisition financing and terms. The best acquisition will largely pay for itself from the target company's own earnings. Properly structured, this can often be done and still meet the price requirements of the seller.

In any acquisition, either a known target or one from a search in a new market area, just look for these three elements. If they're all in place, your external expansion through acquisition is likely to be successful. If they're not, make sure you address any deficiencies before you embark on an acquisition strategy.

When discussing acquisitions with my clients, I frequently talk about my 95% Rule. That is, 95% or more of the companies in the U.S. are run with the single objective of generating compensation for the owners. The typical example is a husband and wife who own and operate a small convenience store. They work for themselves, make an adequate living, and don't ask for more.

Five percent or less of U.S. companies are run to build value. Those 5% will eventually acquire many of the other 95%. Although managing a company to build value and using acquisitions as one method of accomplishing that goal requires somewhat different management tasks and expertise, building value and maximizing personal compensation are not incompatible. Building value will usually lead to increased compensation not only for the company owners but also for its managers and other employees.

In assessing the options for the growth of your company, acquisitions, mergers, or other forms of external growth should be a major consideration. After all, in the U.S. markets, there are companies that are growing and companies that are shrinking. There are few, if any, companies which can remain stagnant for an extended period of time. Explore whether you can or should pursue external growth for your company as a means of assuring that it is not stagnant or losing market share and shrinking.

By the way, you might be interested that I wrote another book which was published in late 2006. It is _Let's Buy a Company: How to Accelerate Growth Through Acquisitions_. Although long out of print, that book can usually be bought used through Amazon.com. It is principally a step-by-step manual for the entire acquisition process. It also includes a Workbook section on CD-ROM with actual examples of forms, proposals, Letters of Intent, and various spreadsheets for financial analysis, price calculations, and debt service coverage all related to acquisitions.

83

Chapter 31 - Customer Communications

A mong the more important communications for any company are its communications with its customers. Those can take many direct and indirect forms. For instance, print and other media advertising is an indirect form of customer communication. You place an ad where it is likely to be seen by the intended audience, hope they will respond, and then attempt to determine if the ad was cost effective. (Also see Chapter 11.)

A letter or e-mail to all of your current customers advising them of a new product or service is a direct form of customer communication. Also, sending such a letter or e-mail to individual prospective customers broadens its reach and usually its effect on sales.

Start today to compile a list of all the methods you now use to communicate with your customers as well as those which are available but not currently used. Divide that list into direct and indirect categories and add notes as to how effective each method might be and what each might cost. Then refine that list over time as you try various forms of customer communication and measure their effect on sales, customer retention, new customer generation, and customer awareness of your company and its products or services. That list can also be used to allocate advertising and other marketing expenses to those techniques which are the most cost effective.

What many company managers don't consider is that customer communications should, wherever possible, include facilities for dialogue in both directions. Giving your customers the ability to communicate easily with your company is one of the most important forms of contact with that important constituency.

You might, for instance, use a company website as one method of promoting feedback from your current and prospective customers. In addition to presenting your company and its products or services, your website should also be interactive. Your customers and other site visitors should be able to send questions, comments, complaints, or suggestions directly from the site back to appropriate people at your company.

Other forms of communications from your customers back to your company include telephone conversations with your customer service representatives, comment cards sent with ordered products, or follow-up calls after a product has been received or a service provided. It's not good enough that you think you know how your customers feel about your company. You should know exactly what they think. You can't do that if they don't tell you, and they aren't likely to tell you if they don't have an easy and convenient method of doing so.

In addition, for all communications from your customers, be sure they are answered promptly and appropriately. Having a customer complaint or suggestion go unanswered is one of the worst mistakes you can make with customer communications.

In regard to measuring the effect of your various forms of customer communications, your service representatives or salespeople should always ask, when contacted by a new customer, how and where they heard about your company.

You should then keep records of those responses and use that data to direct your marketing efforts toward the most effective media and methods. You should also measure the frequency and extent of your customer communications. Every member of your sales group should submit weekly customer call reports. You'll not only know which of your salespeople are working the hardest but can also measure their closing rate or revenue generation.

Lots of salespeople can make lots of sales calls but not generate much revenue. To prevent that, all of your salespeople should clearly understand the difference between presenting a product or service and asking for the order. (Also see Chapter 6.)

Periodic call reports are even more important for independent sales representatives. Because most of those sales agencies carry multiple lines, you should know how often and to whom your products or services are presented. You can then measure closing rates and compare the efficiency of your sales reps based on their communications with potential customers. I've often heard that independent sales agents use their independence to resist compiling and sending sales call reports. In my experience, however, if those agents won't send call reports, you probably have the wrong representatives. (Also see Chapters 6 and 53.)

In addition, as one part of their customer communications, your sales group, whether employees or agents, should maintain an up-to-date, computer based list of all customer and prospect contact information. The salespeople should be able to enter a new name in the list or change the contact information with computer access from any location. In addition to name, address, and phone number, the list should also include e-mail addresses.

There are a number of commercial software programs designed specifically to manage sales prospect and customer data. Just do an internet search for "sales management software" to see available products and related websites.

For many companies, a particularly effective method of customer communications is a monthly newsletter sent by e-mail. I've long found that to be an excellent method of reminding my past and prospective clients of my corporate finance and consulting services. To review various software packages for sending multiple e-mails, do an internet search for "broadcast e-mail software".

By the way, sending any customer communication without having it addressed to a specific person by name is a big mistake. A letter addressed to "occupant", to "the President", or to only the company name will be discarded, and the postage, paper, and time spent on the letter will all be wasted. An e-mailed newsletter not individually addressed to a person by name is spam, and we all know what happens to that.

Customer memories are short. Don't let your customers or prospects forget that your company is active, interested in addressing their needs, and sensitive to their feelings about your products or services. Communicate with your customers frequently and consistently.

Chapter 32 - The Merry-Go-Round

I had a visit from my friend Al B. Rich a month or so ago. I had seen Al last year just after he completed the concept design for an internet B2B portal for buyers of eye glass hinges and screws. I had explained then that the internet bubble had burst some years ago costing many investors I know a good portion of their retirement funds. Now Al was back to relate his experiences in The Money Search.

His first stop had been the bookstore which cheerfully supplied 16 volumes on how to write a business plan, attract venture capital, and live a life of idle wealth. I glanced out the window and noticed that Al had traded his Porsche Boxster for a 2005 Ford with a little rust under the door. As we talked, I turned to the marketing section of his two hundred page "Private Placement Offering Memorandum and Disclaimer", the disclaimers added at great expense by his lawyer. As usual, "Marketing" started with the astounding statistic that there are 300 million people in the U.S. Once this population had been distilled down to the eye glass wearers, companies that supply them, and the 10% market share Al's B2B exchange would attract, his projected third year sales were a conservative $78.6 million with a 16% after tax margin. I could easily see how everyone was going to get rich; instead I think most of them got Rich.

He had sent the Plan to 36 venture capital firms and 12 SBIC's listed in the free state development office directory of money sources. That was the only item Al got for free. Nine of the VC's responded that they were putting his Plan in their files pending further market developments. Four SBIC's passed it on to people they knew in the industry for evaluation. Fifty follow-up calls later, Al found that those experts passed the Plan on to more specialized experts until they found one who knew enough to kill the idea.

But one venture capitalist wanted to talk. Never mind that he was not on the list or that his address was the South Bronx, Al gladly spent $1,289 for a first class (he might sit next to an investor) ticket to New York. Maybe he should have wondered when the meeting was at O'Mally's Italian Diner and Al picked up the check, but this guy controlled millions. Most of the conversation, however, concerned the New Yorker's search for distressed Florida hotels that could be bought for no money down with 100% financing. Al couldn't help him, and he couldn't help Al.

However, it wasn't a wasted trip; Al stopped in to see Monnie Dodge, an old friend who had done tax shelters way back in the '90's. Dodge still couldn't believe that game was over. He could, he explained, package Al's deal as an intellectual property partnership. Al would still own 100% of his company and just pay royalties to the partners. Converting the Business Plan

87

into the Partnership Offering only cost $5,000 up front to Dodge plus twenty grand to the lawyers and a minor $7,500 for new financial projections. Oh, Al also remembered the $5,634 tax opinion and the $678 for FedEx delivery, the only mailing service those lawyers knew existed. If Dodge didn't know the tax shelter partnership game was over, he found out on Al's deal and then joined his brother-in-law's Roto-Rooter franchise.

After that debacle, a friend of Al's introduced him to a guy in Miami who controlled South American money. Forget that Gonzales Sneed had blond hair and an office in a three floor walk-up, the deal sounded enticing. His client would lend Al $50 million; Al would deposit $43 million in a Cayman Island bank and pay for the balance at 4-3/4% over prime, repayable in six months with roll-over privileges and convertibility if his company was a success. That exercise only cost Al $7,500 to Sneed, a bargain when you compare it to the partnership deal.

There was, however, a new venture incubation center opening right near Al's home office. Everything a budding company could need was provided, including a state development officer as a consultant. For only $4,000 a month Al got an office, copy machine, secretarial service, phone, and free coffee between ten and two. He virtually lived there before he discovered that the new venture incubation center had everything except a source of development capital, the one item a new venture needs before all others.

The development officer did, however, introduce Al to four venture capital clubs and got his Plan accepted for a high-tech enterprise forum where capitalists and entrepreneurs meet to exchange money for stock. Al made presentations to the clubs in front of accountants, deal packagers, other hopefuls, and office supply salesmen but few, if any, investors. Regardless, Al didn't win any of the beauty contests.

At that point, he was getting desperate so he finally visited the High-Tech Pawnbroker and Financing Authority in Ft. Lauderdale. "Welcome", said the unctuous man behind the counter, "so you want to start a high-tech company; I've got the money, but it ain't cheap."

"Right," responded Al, "for just a million I'll give you 10% and a seat on the board."

"Just a minute, I'm the guy with the money; I'll set the terms. I'll give you $50,000 now for 40% and two board seats. If it works and I approve your business plan, you get another $100,000; I get another 30%, two more seats, and meanwhile I drive your Porsche. That's a generous deal."

"But that's not enough," said Al quietly. "How about my house; it's gotta be worth $250,000."

The man, who happened to be a real estate broker on the side, was quick to answer, "Hundred grand, my best offer, and how about your watch. I pay top dollar for Rolexes."

Is there a better way? I tried to tell Al about market research and management teams, structuring the financing for the target investor, and using an expert's knowledge of the capital markets. "But wait," said Al, "I've scrapped the internet portal idea and developed a new video game that plays automatically every time your cell phone rings..."

Raising growth capital for any company is difficult. It should be done, however, with a good presentation of only pertinent historical, market and financial information directed toward reasonable capital sources related to the company's markets, status, and potential. Even then, over the years, I have found that raising startup funds for a high risk venture is almost, but sometimes not quite, impossible.

Chapter 33 - Corporate Reputation

I recently read in The Wall Street Journal that "corporate reputation is a means to success, not a by-product of that success." That reminded me of a quote by James Russell Lowell, an American writer and diplomat in the late 1800's, who said, "Reputation is only a candle, of wavering and uncertain flame, and easily blown out, but it is the light by which the world looks for and finds merit."

Companies over time, often a surprisingly short period of time, attract a certain reputation in their markets. Once established for the better, however, that reputation can quickly change for the worse and then be particularly difficult to correct. Your company's reputation can be one of its most valuable assets and is one you should guard as carefully as you do a patented or proprietary design. In addition, you can, and should, exert a significant influence over the reputation by which your company is known.

First, however, you must know what that reputation is. That's relatively easy to determine: just ask. But don't ask only your customers, include your competitors' customers, as well as your suppliers and your employees. You can use a mailed or e-mailed questionnaire for each of those groups, although your response rate may be somewhat low. That rate will depend, among other factors, on how your cover letter is phrased and the time it takes to complete the questionnaire.

For a mailed questionnaire, you should always include a stamped, return envelope. I've also received such questionnaires that enclosed a new dollar bill as thanks for taking the time to respond. One dollar isn't much, but I was more inclined to answer after receiving it.

You might also have those people at your company in contact with each of its various constituents call them or include the questionnaire with their other contacts. Your purchasing agents would handle the suppliers; your salespeople would talk with their customers, and each department manager would talk with their employees. For your competitors' customers, have your salespeople call them. Those contacts, and the fact that you're interested in understanding and improving your reputation, might even lead to new customer relationships.

Another method of determining your company's reputation is to engage a marketing consultant. Work with that consultant to develop an appropriate questionnaire for each constituency and give them the contact information they need to canvas each group. An unaffiliated consultant will often receive answers that might not be given to a member of your company.

At a minimum, your questionnaire should include the perception of your company in regard its quality of goods or services; the attitude of its

90

employees; its response to orders, questions, and problems; its prices; its delivery times and methods; its warranty policies; and the overall feeling toward your company taken as a whole. In addition, it is always good to ask how your company might improve any aspect of its products or services.

There should, of course, be different questions for each different group. For your employees, for instance, there should be a question regarding internal communications. For your suppliers, you should question their feelings regarding your payment policies and how their relationship with your company compares to their other customers.

Whether conducted by your own managers or by a consultant, the results of that study should be condensed into a report given to every member of your company's management group. That group should then meet to discuss any deficiencies and how those deficiencies should and could be corrected. Reputations are long lived and, unfortunately, bad reputations are longer lived than good ones.

Several years ago, I compiled a five year Strategic Plan for a client company selling technical equipment used in a particular recreational sport. Among the users of its equipment, the company had a reputation for exceptional quality. Among its retail dealer customers, however, it had attracted a reputation for slow deliveries, incorrect orders, and relatively poor customer service. We were able to use its reputation for quality as a means of maintaining those relationships with its dealers while the company addressed its delivery problems. It took time, but today that company's reputation for delivery to its customers is high and its reputation with its end users for quality equipment also remains high. It has a good reputation with both of those important groups.

Once you know your company's reputation with each of its constituents, you can then work to improve it. Even if your reputation is high in most, if not all categories, there are always improvements that can be made. You can't make them, however, if you don't know what that reputation is.

Because I started this Chapter with two quotations, I'll end with another. Several centuries ago, Socrates said, "The way to gain a good reputation is to endeavor to be what you desire to appear." That's as true for companies as it is for individuals. You have more control over your corporate reputation than you might imagine, but you must exert that control and make sure your company's reputation is one of its principal assets and not a liability.

91

Chapter 34 - Performance Reviews

W e've talked previously about the hiring process and methods you can use to attract good people to your company (Chapters 2 and 27) . Once those people are in place, however, you should also measure their performance in various ways and use the results to make sure the person is well suited to the job and, equally as important, that the job is well suited to the person. More often than you might think a job description, level of responsibility, or lines of communication can be changed to turn a marginal employee into an exceptional one. In most cases, people want to do a good job and will work toward that objective if given an appropriate opportunity.

One element of making such job adjustments is an understanding with the employee as to their job performance and how it might be improved. A difficult and often neglected part of managing any organization is a periodic discussion with each person under your direction as to their job performance. Particularly where there are problems, those conversations are too easy to avoid. They can, however, be vitally important to the smooth and efficient operation of any organization.

In the case of many closely held companies, job performance reviews with the owners' family members can be even more difficult than with others but are as necessary as any, and perhaps more so. By having a formal job review process, there are no excuses for treating a family member differently than any other employee or neglecting to tell that person that he or she could and should improve. (Also see Chapter 28.)

Employee performance reviews should be a requirement for all managers and should be scheduled on a regular six month or annual basis. Each manager should develop a questionnaire for those reviews that is appropriate to the position being discussed. The manager should also take notes regarding his or her conversation with the employees under their direction and put a written report in each individual's personnel file.

It is particularly important that the report include negative as well as positive comments. Because it's easier to discuss successes rather than failures and good performance rather than bad, too many performance reviews neglect those areas which need improvement or might subsequently be a basis for demotion or dismissal if not corrected.

Important areas that should be covered with each employee include:

- their communications and relationships with other employees, both above and below their position in the company;

- your perception and their own feelings about their job performance;

- how their job might be changed to better suit their personal strengths;

- their feelings about the company and its other employees;
- attendance issues;
- their compensation;
- the aspects of their job which they most enjoy and those they dislike;
- their career objectives and what they might need to do to reach those objectives within your company;
- and of course, any specific areas related to their job performance that need to be improved.

Periodic performance reviews will often result in improvements by the employees who better understand how their immediate superiors view their performance. In today's litigious world, such performance reviews, if properly conducted and recorded, can also be excellent insurance against employee litigation or other disputes regarding either termination, promotions, or compensation.

In regard to those discussions with each employee, there are several software programs that can be used to format and assist with the interviews. They can be found with an internet search using the key words "employee performance management" or "employee performance reviews".

Maintaining current and consistent personnel files for all company employees, including performance reviews, is an important part of the human resource function at any company. In addition to formal procedures for reviewing job performance and the maintenance of the personnel files, all companies should also have written procedures for any employee termination, either voluntary or involuntary.

We often think of such termination procedures only for an employee being fired. It is equally important, however, to understand why an employee decides to move from your company to another. In any instance of any employee quitting their job, their immediate supervisor and the HR manager should arrange an exit interview and use that conversation to determine what caused the employee to either look for or accept another position. On occasion, those interviews can result in having the employee change their mind. At the least, an understanding as to their rationale for leaving can be used to keep other employees who might follow them for similar reasons.

Of course, the exit interview for a fired employee is particularly important not just as litigation insurance. It should also be used to make sure the employee understands why the action has been taken. Other than avoiding litigation, a mutual discussion and understanding as to why an employee has been fired can often defuse negative feelings toward the company and inappropriate comments by the terminated employee either inside or outside the company.

93

In addition, the exit interview should be used to be sure the fired employee understands their obligations regarding the company's intellectual property and any confidentiality or noncompetition provisions outlined in the company's employee handbook or in any employment contract with the person.

Employee performance reviews and exit interviews can be difficult. Few people enjoy discussing such issues. They should, however, be as much a part of corporate procedures as facility operations, safety issues, and administrative functions, among others. Making such reviews and interviews a regular and mandatory part of your company's operations will not only make them easier to conduct but can also make them a valuable source of information for both the company and its employees.

Chapter 35 - Don't Steal From Yourself

D on't steal from yourself. That sounds silly, but it's what I call hiding personal income among business expenses. When selling companies for my clients, I'm always concerned when I hear that the actual profits are higher than those reported to the IRS.

First, a tax audit will usually uncover such hidden income and result in penalties and interest far in excess of the earlier benefits you thought you enjoyed. Second, no corporate nor most individual buyers for a company will include all of such hidden income in their calculation of an appropriate purchase price.

Because most of that hidden income is excluded, the purchase price is lower, usually much lower, than what the business owners would otherwise have received. And third, knowingly reporting inaccurate income is a felony for which people can and do go to jail. Not a good idea.

Paying the IRS is a high class problem. It means you're operating a profitable enterprise on which taxes on those profits are due. When not paying the IRS what is due, you're either operating a losing business or you're cheating in ways you shouldn't. If losses are the reason for the lack of tax obligations, you need to correct the profit problems fast. If cheating is the reason for the lack of tax obligations, or just taxes lower than you should pay, you're operating a criminal enterprise. Sounds ominous, but it's factual.

Those warnings relate to taxes on income. Accurately calculating and paying those taxes is extremely important. Paying taxes on payroll, however, and paying those taxes on a timely basis, is not just important, it's imperative.

To the Internal Revenue Service, payroll taxes are in a unique category. Withholding, social security, and Medicare taxes are monies that do not, and have never, belonged to the company or person making the payments. Those funds are, and from their inception always were, the property of the Federal Government. Not remitting those payroll taxes on a timely basis can result in draconian actions on the part of the IRS, and those actions can be taken immediately.

In addition to holding all company directors, any officers with signature power over a bank account, and the accounting managers personally responsible for any and all unpaid payroll taxes, the IRS can use that unmet responsibility to seize both corporate and personal bank accounts. In regard to other company assets, an IRS lien for unpaid payroll taxes is superior to any other loans, including secured bank loans. Your friendly tax collector can padlock the door to your facility and claim the assets. I've seen it happen.

Several years ago, when I was just starting a turn-around effort for a chronically unprofitable company, the owner called one morning to tell me that the IRS had closed the plant. The IRS agent actually put a new hasp and lock on the front door with no prior notice. That was the first I learned of the unpaid payroll taxes. We were able to negotiate with the IRS agent and reopen, but it took several days as well as a significant payment against the past due taxes, interest, and penalties that was particularly difficult to make.

The problem for companies with insufficient working capital is the ease with which the IRS can become a source of borrowed funds. No need to fill out loan applications; a history of continuing losses is not a problem; just don't pay the payroll taxes and use those funds to support the business. When that starts, it's always a short term loan. Too often, it then becomes a long term loan but can quickly convert to a short term problem.

At that point, the unpaid FICA and other payroll taxes become more of a threat to your business than any other factor. Borrowing the payroll taxes is the worst source of funds for any company. If such borrowings are ever necessary, the company has problems that should have been solved earlier and in another fashion.

The rules are easy to follow: For all payroll taxes, pay the IRS first, no exceptions. For all income related taxes, calculate the income accurately and pay the taxes when due.

My own business is a sole proprietorship operated from a home office, but I keep financial records as if it were a much larger corporation. That is particularly true for all of those items subject to fudging. For example, every time I visit a client, I record my mileage and apply the standard IRS allowed mileage charge for that year.

Each month, I submit that mileage record to my wife for payment. She keeps a separate bank account for Florida Corporate Finance, my sole proprietorship, and never mingles either income or expenses with our house accounts. At the end of each month, she reimburses the house accounts for the mileage charges and any other expenses paid from the house accounts during that month.

Any business owner or executive should keep similar records of all business related expenses paid by their company which could be personal. Any personal expenses, should be paid by the individual and not by the company. If any such expenses are paid by the company, the owner or executive should write a check to reimburse the company. Doing otherwise is playing Russian roulette with the IRS, and in that game, the IRS always wins.

When developing Strategic Plans for my client companies, I always advise them to keep all of their options open. Among those are a possible sale or other form of corporate relationship for their company.

Although a sale of the company may be out in some indefinite future, you never know. An attractive buyer might surface or the owner's heirs may be the sellers long before he or she planned. In any case, the value of the company will usually be based principally on its history of earnings. If those earnings are artificially low due to tax games, the price will also be low.

I'll say it one more time, "Pay the IRS first." You'll never regret following that simple policy.

97

Chapter 36 - Debt Financing

There are few companies that can operate without some source of external financing which is often used to support its working capital or additional growth. Knowing the sources, costs, and feasibility of arranging such financing can be an important element in any company's growth plans and, on occasion, its survival. Of course, the best known and most widely available source of such operating capital is a local bank. For debt financing, bank loans are also the least expensive. Banks, however, are generally "cash flow" lenders. That is, they lend to companies that are operating profitably and have a relatively high debt service coverage (principal plus interest) provided by their operating cash flow.

The two primary forms of bank debt are credit lines and term loans. In general, credit lines are short term borrowings for working capital purposes and are used to support fluctuations in the principal components of that working capital, that is, accounts receivable and inventories.

The credit line borrowing base and outstanding amount changes as the levels of those two current assets change. The interest rates for credit lines are also usually variable and change with market rates from the prime rate as a low up to three percent or more over prime depending upon the financial strength of the borrower.

Bank term loans are fixed dollar amounts most often used to fund longer term asset purchases such as equipment, vehicles, or acquisitions. Those loans are payable monthly, usually over three to seven years, and can have either fixed or variable interest rates. Those rates are usually equivalent to credit line interest for any given borrower but may be higher for longer term loans.

Although banks talk about asset based lending and will certainly want a first lien security interest in all company assets to secure their loans, they are primarily interested in the profit and cash flow levels needed to assure that their loans will be repaid on a timely basis. True asset based lenders, however, expect the liquidation value of the company's assets to fully secure their loans. Most often those assets based loan sources are referred to as commercial lenders and are not conventional banks.

Those non-bank sources for debt financing will often provide funds to a weaker credit than a bank. Although commercial lenders may provide a loan to a company that is marginally profitable or, on occasion, even unprofitable, they will want to have their loan secured by identified assets that can be relatively easily liquidated in the event of a default. In addition, that liquidation or "midnight sale" value must be sufficient to fully retire the outstanding balance for their loan. Because those assets are most often "near cash" items such as accounts receivable and inventory, most loans from commercial lenders have characteristics similar to bank credit lines.

The total cost of funds charged by commercial lenders, however, is usually significantly higher than the interest on bank loans. In addition to interest on the borrowed funds in the range of prime plus two to six percent, commercial lenders also charge a number of fees that can increase the effective interest rate or total cost of funds to a range of 12% to as much as 18%. Those fees include quarterly field audits during which an auditor for the lender spends several days at the borrower's facility confirming the accounts receivable, inventory levels, and other assets in relation to the borrowing base calculations used to establish the amount of allowable funding. Those audit fees can be $800 to $1,000 per day plus travel expenses.

In addition, commercial lenders often charge an annual facility fee of 1% or so of the total funds available, whether used or not, plus monthly servicing costs of 0.1% to 0.2% or more of the average outstanding balance during the month. Early termination fees of 1% to 3% of the total credit facility can also add to the expenses associated with a loan from a commercial lender All of those various fees become part of the effective interest or the cost of funds for the borrower.

The least attractive form of debt financing is factoring. That is generally the sale of accounts receivable to a "factor" for some discounted amount. Although the account receivable is paid to the borrower by the factor within days of the related sale, if your company averages a collection period of 45 days and you sell your receivables to a factor for a 3% discount, that is equivalent to an annual interest rate of 24%. The effective interest rate for factored receivables can often be as high as 36% per year or more.

Factoring was originally designed for use by garment manufacturers which sold goods to department stores that demanded 120 day payment terms. Because the manufacturers enjoyed relatively high gross profits and had long collection periods, they could afford to discount their receivables to a factor. However, for other manufacturers or distributors with lower gross profits and shorter collection periods, selling receivables to a factor is not usually an attractive source of funds. I often tell my clients that when factoring their receivables, they end up working for the factor and not for themselves.

Beyond those forms of debt financing, there are also several sources of equity financing for private companies. Those include venture capital firms, "angels", corporate investors, and individuals, among others. I'll discuss equity financing in more detail in Chapter 49. In general, however, any form of equity financing, such as the sale of a common stock interest in your company, is usually much more difficult to arrange than debt. Such equity financing is used when the growth capital needed by a company is significantly higher than any amount it might borrow from conventional

99

sources. In cases where the sale of equity is being considered because a company's financial condition is too poor to support debt financing, it's usually best to cure the financial results problem prior to raising any new funds from any sources.

On occasion, I've had clients point with pride at a balance sheet devoid of any credit line or long term debt. My usual response is that such a balance sheet shows a deficiency in the use of the company's assets to support additional or accelerated growth. If a company has excessive financial strength, its owners and managers should determine how to use that strength to increase the revenues, profits, and enterprise value of their company. Excessive financial strength is, to me, as much an indicator of management weakness as excessively poor performance.

Chapter 37 - Working for Yourself

S everal years ago, I arranged the sale of a small company to an executive who had always wanted to own a company and work for himself. Unfortunately, he came from a background that included a variety of positions with significantly larger operations where, in each case, he managed a staff of people. He was a great manager but not used to doing virtually all of the work himself.

After acquiring his new company, he attempted to add personnel faster than its profits could support. He spent money on marketing that would have been routine for a larger operation but was not cost effective for his. After several years of losses, the company he bought failed. He found that wanting to own a company and actually doing it were quite different. It was an expensive lesson.

Throughout my corporate finance consulting career, I've worked with many entrepreneurs. I've also talked with many individuals who dreamed of owning a company, and I've seen others attempt to purchase a job by buying a company. In all of those cases, unless the company's new owner clearly understood the demands and the work that would be required, his or her ownership often turned into a drastic mistake. That certainly doesn't mean that failure is the most probable outcome from owning a business; it is only a note of caution in what is too often a dream that is not based on reality.

Owning a company, and being successful at it, requires a combination of skills as well as a passion for the business that could be used as a definition for the word "entrepreneur". Before you embark on such a venture, make sure you're ready and able to devote the hours of work, the dedication to your market, and the capital funds needed for success. Then make sure you have the skills necessary for addressing the numerous problems you and your company will face. Also, in a small company environment, make sure you can and will do it yourself rather than asking some subordinate who won't be there to do it for you.

In regard to capital requirements, I've often told entrepreneurs how to calculate the working capital and other funds needed to support either an acquisition or a start-up. After converting income statement projections into balance sheets and then into a cash flow analysis, the capital needs should be well defined. I then tell my clients to double the amount shown by such calculations because that is what they will really need.

Of course, not all entrepreneurs face insurmountable problems. Not too long ago, I helped a young manager acquire a small company which manufacturers high performance, after market, motorcycle parts. He knew nothing about motorcycles, didn't even own one, and had never attended a

101

motorcycle race. He did, however, have a solid background in metal fabrication and machining, the same processes used in making motorcycle parts.

Of equal importance, he had previously worked for several small companies with small staffs and had been involved in sales as well as management for those companies. He had the skills needed to control a small operation with few people around him, and he knew how to organize the work flow in a metal fabrication shop. He also believed he could quickly learn how to maintain and increase sales to motorcycle enthusiasts. He was right, and his new business prospered.

He did, however, work about sixty to seventy hours a week for the first year and spent numerous nights in relatively down-scale hotels and motels while attending motorcycle events and trade shows. He learned the motorcycle markets, reorganized his manufacturing operation to improve the production efficiencies, and added financial controls that allowed him and his few supervisors to identify problems quickly and then solve them. He is an entrepreneur, and it shows.

He also chose his target carefully. He knew that he did not want to own a metal working job shop that competes almost exclusively on price for each project. Instead, he wanted a metal working facility producing proprietary products which could be priced with a higher gross margin and sold into a much wider geographic market than job shop projects. High performance motorcycle parts turned out to be a particularly good candidate.

By the way, in regard to starting your own business or buying one, the statistics for success are weighted heavily toward acquisitions. Rather than fight for market share against well entrenched competition, buy one of those competitors and start with an existing market presence. In addition, the capital needs for an acquisition, including working capital to support growth, are much easier to estimate than the needs for a startup. Working capital needs, however, are still subject to my doubling suggestion.

But what if you aren't an entrepreneur or don't have the urge or determination to own and manage your own company? You can still benefit from the suggestions in both this chapter and this book. On a periodic basis, evaluate the business of the company for which you work as if you were thinking of buying it. Review its markets and how they might be expanded. Attempt to value the company and then think about how that value might be increased in the future. Evaluate the business risks associated with the company and its markets and think about how those risks could be minimized or eliminated.

Think like an entrepreneur, even if you aren't one. Your contribution to your company and its level of success will both increase.

102

Chapter 38 - Losses: Cure Them Now

If your company is losing money, do something about it and do it immediately. That might seem like a plainly evident, even stupid, statement, but you would be surprised how many executives don't follow that simple rule. I developed a Strategic Plan for a client company several years ago with a serious purchasing and inventory control problem. Hundred dollar products sat for weeks waiting for a part that cost fifty cents.

For several years, that company vacillated between breakeven and small losses while its management team discussed the "inventory" problem but did nothing to cure it. In fact, the solution was simple. I suggested enclosing the parts inventory and hiring a warehouseman who would have sole access to the stores. We also set up minimum order quantities based on the rate of parts use and their delivery schedules.

When I made those suggestions, I was told that the company could not afford another employee to man the parts stores. However, the production efficiencies from this simple change more than paid for the warehouseman and allowed the company to generate consistent rather than sporadic profits.

Years ago, my father told me, "A company with a tax loss carry forward is a proven loser". He was right.

At the first sign of a loss or even declining profit margins, figure out what is happening and why. Start by determining whether the change in performance is caused by internal or external factors.

If a profit problem is internal, it may even be easy to identify and solve, but first you must have the information needed to find it. I'm always amazed when I see income statements for either manufacturing or service companies with one line for Direct Costs and fifty lines for G&A expenses.

In manufacturing there are no more important statistics than direct labor and direct material costs as a percent of sales and per unit of production. In service companies, the various components of Direct Costs and their relation to revenues are also principal determinants of profitability. Without those measures, how can you determine the source of eroding gross profits?

If gross profits are stable but net profits are falling, examine your G&A expenses as a percent of sales and then look at the trend for the major G&A line items over the past six to twelve months. Where there are anomalies, find the cause and take corrective action, but not tomorrow; do it today.

If there has been no significant change in your direct, indirect, or G&A expenses as a percent of sales, the problem must be external. Prices could be eroding due to competitive pressures or because the wrong people can control prices (salespeople, for example) and are looking at maximizing revenue rather than profits. Perhaps a new competitor has entered the market and is taking market share from your company or a technological advance has put your products or services at a competitive disadvantage.

Whatever the external problem might be, identify it. Only then can you determine how the threat might be addressed, how long that might take, and what the cost will be, including the support for continued losses or lower margins while the remedy is put in place. Even in the face of intractable market problems, there is always a solution, but without knowing what the problem is, you can't address it.

An extreme example is the disappearance of the radio vacuum tube market. In the first half of the last century, replacement vacuum tubes could be purchased at most hardware stores using testers to determine the pin spacing and what part number was needed. There were several dozen companies in the U.S. producing those radio tubes. But then the transistor was introduced.

The radio tube market simply evaporated, although that took a number of years. Today, however, there is one company left still producing radio vacuum tubes for hobbyist and collectors of radios, Victrolas, and early TV's. That one company figured out how to maintain its profits in a declining market and is still quite profitable, although much smaller than it was eighty years ago.

I've too often seen companies which were, in fact, insolvent but continued to operate for an incredible number of years. They borrowed from their suppliers, refinanced rather than retired loans, factored their receivables, and continued to kid themselves into believing that their problems would correct themselves over time. They wouldn't, didn't, and eventually resulted in liquidation.

Minor losses can usually be sustained for a long period of time, but that is no reason to allow them to continue.

Another of my past clients in the transportation business began to experience periodic losses with returns to profits and then more losses. When the decision was finally made to find and correct the problem, the first step was to dissect each business function at the company and examine its contribution to profits or losses.

By segregating the various contributors revenues and then computing their relative contributions to overhead, it was found that losses occurred when the custom packing revenues were highest and trucking revenues were lowest. The custom packing operation was a consistent loser that was hidden by the profits from trucking. A minor increase in custom packing prices which, by the way, were less price sensitive than hauling freight, was combined with an improvement in packing efficiencies to cure the problem.

A little loss is usually a symptom of a bigger problem. Untreated, it can place the health, and even the existence, of your company at risk. Don't lose sight of those symptoms, and once found, go to work on a solution right now.

105

Is This Any Way to Run a Company?   H. Lee Rust

Chapter 39 - One Bad Apple

How bad can one person be? Just one can be bad enough to cripple or even destroy a company of some significant size. A few years ago, I had a client with over $50 million of annual sales and several subsidiaries which showed consistent profits. It did, however, have an incompetent accounting manager, CPA certification notwithstanding. On several occasions, I pointed out not only deficiencies in the monthly reporting but also blatant errors. In addition, the monthly statements were never available until at least six weeks after each close. The company's principals, however, were good construction managers but certainly not accountants. They thought they didn't need timely financial reports; they knew what was going on with the field work.

Unfortunately, I was not the only person who recognized a problem. The company's bank finally withdrew its credit line, simply saying that they no longer believed the company's financial reporting was accurate. That not only removed the company's source of working capital but also eliminated its project bonding capacity. After two attempts to quickly replace that key manager and bring the financial reporting up to date, the company was finally sold some months later for about a quarter of its former value.

Don't think it can't happen to you. It's not good enough that you think you know your company's financial health. You must have accounting data that shows it, and you must be able to demonstrate that strength to others, including bankers and often major suppliers and customers.

Although he eventually had plenty of accomplices, Andrew Fastow at Enron Corporation brought down that Fortune 100 company. He was the one with the initial ideas for off-balance sheet partnerships to hide losses and also reaped millions of dollars from his personal participation in those partnerships. Only after he started that process did others at Enron join in both the deceptions and the illicit rewards.

A few years later, Enron ceased to exist. It also, by the way, destroyed the fourth largest accounting firm in the U.S. due to the complacency of a singe Houston based audit partner involved in the Enron deceptions.

We all know stories of the accountant or bookkeeper who begins to "borrow" money from their company. Some years ago, the owner of a company that manufactured plastic sign lettering and was a client of mine noticed that his CFO was driving an automobile that was way beyond his salary level. It was too late; the embezzlement was too large and the doctored financial statements had gone on too long. The company was liquidated.

And another client started a new venture in a remote state based on the talents of a single person who was to manage the new operation. My client, however, was too busy with his Florida operation to supervise a small company in the Carolinas. After a loss of $1.7 million and multiple law suits later, that operation was closed but had virtually crippled its Florida parent. The creation of that loss took less than eighteen months. The parent company had been in business for eighteen years.

That's how bad one person can be, but what are the remedies? First, timely, accurate, and understandable financial statements. If your company's monthly income statements and balance sheets aren't on the desk of all managers by the fifteenth of the following month, they are an historical curiosity and not an adequate control tool. If they can't be completed by the fifteenth, change the accounting procedures or the person responsible for producing them.

That, however, is not enough. Question any item that appears to be unreasonable, widely fluctuating, or simply wrong. In fact, it's a good idea to periodically take a single income statement or balance sheet line item and review all of the source data back to original invoices. Hopefully, you won't find anything amiss, but your accounting personnel will know you're looking.

Also, as I've said previously, have your annual financial statements audited. Certainly, that costs more than a review or the virtually worthless compilation. The extra cost, however, is more than repaid by the increase in enterprise value for a company with fully audited statements and your knowledge that a more rigorous examination of your financial controls will take place each year.

If you have a company with more than one employee, require that there be two signatures on any check. For checks over a specified size, require that one of those signatures be a company officer. Two people can collaborate to steal from a company, but it's a lot harder, a lot more complex, and much less likely if there are two signatures on all company checks.

In addition, review the security provisions in your accounting software. Many small companies use QuickBooks, the almost universal beginning accounting package. The original QuickBooks, however, lacked an adequate audit trail and, even worse, allowed changes to individual entries well after a month's close and did not record such changes.

Other than accounting, financial, and cash controls, also examine any other company function that can result in unforeseen or potential losses. Project estimates and bids should always be reviewed by at least one person who is not responsible for preparing them. Scrap sale procedures and receipts should be carefully monitored. And a periodic review of all vendors to your company should include questions as to any vendor name that is not familiar.

In the late 90's, I had a client in the wholesale petroleum products distribution business. As means of smoothing the effects of volatility in oil prices, his COO developed a system of hedging in the gasoline futures

107

markets. On several occasions, I urged the owner of that company to request and check e-mailed duplicate trade confirmations. You can guess the rest of the story. After months of buying and selling futures contracts, the COO had a feel for the market fluctuations. After a big loss, he doubled his bet in a period when price should have risen, but that also turned out to be wrong. Several days later, that company lost $250,000 in about ten minutes. Several months later, I was working to sell what was left.

You and your management team have worked hard to build your company. Don't let one bad person strip the value from all of that work. Finally, don't think it can't happen to you. With all of the examples sited above, my clients couldn't believe that it had happened to them, but it did.

Chapter 40 - Websites

Because of the importance of the internet to any business, I thought another chapter on websites would be warranted. You would have to be dead or living in one of the world's most remote locations not to have noticed the changes the internet has imposed on all businesses. Retail sales on the web increase at a rate we couldn't have imagined a few years ago. Instant news is replacing the daily newspaper, even now for local events. Music downloads have changed the way teens buy the latest songs. Corporate communications have migrated to instant e-mail. And virtually all companies now have corporate websites, from the largest international automotive companies to local restaurants with posted menus.

The great majority of those corporate websites, however, are little more than on-line brochures. Although that might be a good advertisement for your company's goods or services, it does not use most of the functions available on the internet. Your company's website can be one of its competitive advantages, but it can also show a lack of ingenuity, thought, or simple attention as to how you might best use internet communications and functions..

With the internet, you have a relatively new and powerful tool at your disposal. You must now learn how to use it to the maximum extent feasible. In particular, the internet is interactive; it works in both directions, and you can and should take advantage of that.

Start by considering each of your company's constituents and how they might use your website. Those constituents are your customers, employees, suppliers, company owners and, if yours is a publicly owned company, the investment community.

In regard to your customers, what important information might your website give them? One of my clients in the home building business takes digital photos weekly of every house under construction that has been sold. It then posts those on its website with password access for each homeowner who can then watch the construction progress of their house. That has turned out to be a major marketing tool for this homebuilder.

Another of my clients with a large steel fabrication operation posts password accessed progress reports for each of its customers, including project milestones, projected completion dates, shipping schedules and, once shipped, tracking information.

I also have a client providing financing and administrative back office support to temporary staffing companies throughout the U.S. Virtually all of their client communications are internet based. Their temporary staffing clients use the internet to record their work hours each day with those hours posted directly to my client's proprietary software. The software automatically converts that information into both invoicing for their client's customers and salary payments to their client's temporary workers.

Each worker can then be paid by check printed in the client's office, by direct deposit, or by additions to a debit card, all handled over the internet. That client of mine is now expanding into a more complete ASP (Application Service Provider) model which will provide all monthly accounting services for each of its clients over the internet from a single central server.

Ask yourself what information your customers might need which you could provide over the internet in real time and then determine how to do it. You can sell that service as another advantage to dealing with your company.

In regard to your employees, an entire section of your corporate website should be devoted to their needs, including both current and prospective employees. Your website can be a particularly effective platform for a monthly employee newsletter. It can also be the location for the old fashion suggestion box allowing your employees to send confidential comments directly to an appropriate manager. And, of course, the internet can be a particularly effective recruiting tool. In addition to simple contact information and available job postings, your corporate website should have application forms for various positions which can be completed online and sent directly from the site.

I also have several clients who use their corporate websites as training tools. Employees can access pertinent courses, complete the course work on the website, and even receive course grades and certifications. Requirements for periodic safety training can be internet based and track not only each employee's access to that section of the site but also provide safety certifications at various levels.

For your suppliers, you should determine what information could and should be exchanged through your corporate website. One of my clients in the construction field has a complete subcontractor bidding module on their website. A potential subcontractor can download project drawings from the site together with specifications and bills of materials and also submit their project bid from the site. For those subcontractors, the site also has a change order submittal and approval function.

For material suppliers, your shipping schedules, freight tracking, and related communications can be effectively handled over the internet. Those can also include the posting of receiving forms, supplier invoicing, and exception reports. Of course, in the other direction, you can also use your website, or perhaps the website of your supplier, as a material ordering platform.

110

As to the owners of your company, if they are not all officers or employees, you can also have a password protected section of your corporate website for monthly or quarterly reports including the posting of financial statements. In the case of a publicly owned company, any investor, current or prospective, should be able to access all SEC filings, news releases, and other such information directly from your corporate website.

All of these functions, however, are useless unless the appropriate person can find your website easily. For people without an existing relationship to your company, that effort often starts with an internet search using one or more key words. For those potential constituents, you need to be sure that your company is close to the top of the resulting search list. In that regard, there are a large number of consultants who specialize in developing website functions that can effect search list placement. Those are generally referred to as SEO (Search Engine Optimization) consultants   Talk to several of those and determine if you can make changes to your corporate site that will move your search placement up.

I recently had a client which manufactures scuba gear. A search for buoyancy compensators showed their company website but only on the second page of the internet listings. With minor adjustments to their site, they moved to the third posting on the first page. Sales increased.

If your company is not taking full advantage of the internet and all of its capabilities, some of your competitors are. Look at their websites to see what functions you should copy. Use the various functions of your own website on a periodic basis to measure its ease of use and its application for each of your company's constituents. The internet and your corporate website should be among your most important corporate communication tools.

111

Chapter 41 - Market Forces

Not long ago, I had a corporate client which was a relatively large manufacturers' representative for a narrow line of large industrial products. For over two decades that company had prospered. For its owners, it generated modest but consistent revenue growth and a nice stream of profits and personal compensation.

With little warning, however, several subtle changes in technology combined with some manufacturing problems at this client's major supplier resulted in a sales decline which quickly led to losses. Struggling to catch up, my client changed suppliers. The old supplier then engaged a competing sales organization and cut prices as a means of maintaining market share. My client's losses increased.

A new mortgage produced enough working capital to support the continuing losses. Finally, the solution turned out to be the addition of several new product lines, an eventual increase in prices by the competition which couldn't sustain such low margins indefinitely, and a severe reduction in my client's overhead. That company barely avoided bankruptcy but is now profitable and, once again, financially strong.

There were two lessons in that sequence of events. First, don't let a single supplier hold the future of your company hostage to a changing marketplace and, second, don't ever underestimate the importance of market intelligence.

As to the first of these lessons, you've often heard that you shouldn't let any single customer represent more than 25% of your annual sales. Such a customer can hold you hostage to their control over the prosperity of your company. They can dictate prices as the big three U.S. auto makers did to their parts manufacturers during the early 2000's driving a number of those major companies into bankruptcy.

The same is true for your suppliers. If a single source supplier represents a majority of your products, components, or raw materials, a change at that supplier might cripple your company. Why leave the financial health of your company in the hands of another company over which you have no control? Examine the importance of all suppliers to your ability to service your markets. If an interruption of deliveries from any of those suppliers would have devastating results for your company, find additional sources and reduce your dependence on any single company.

As to market intelligence, I can't overemphasize the importance of understanding and, where possible, anticipating changes in your markets which can have an impact, either positive or negative, on your company. The client I mentioned above should have seen and reacted to the changes in technology long before they resulted in a significant decrease in sales. If their principal supplier wasn't maintaining a technological lead, they should have located other suppliers well before the decrease in their sales lead to losses.

Another of my clients is a producer of extreme weather clothing, principally for hunters and others who might be in temperatures as low as minus 60 degrees. Because that is a narrow market with few competitors, that company had prospered for years with little change in their clothing line. With consistent sales and profits, the owners of that company didn't see the minor changes in designs and styles which were introduced by its few competitors. After all, color and style had never mattered before. As sales declined and losses mounted, I was asked to sell the company in what amounted to a liquidation.

The new owner, now a new client of mine, redesigned the line without changing the technology underlying its extreme weather protection. New bright colors in striking designs made the line attractive to snowmobilers and other sportsmen and, in particular, to the women who participate in cold weather sports. The addition of several overseas suppliers reduced the dependence on what had been a single and not always reliable source for the individual outer garments. And several changes in the level of low temperature protection extended the line into the industrial markets for warehouse freezers and North Sea oil platforms, among others. Revenues and profits are now growing again.

Don't be complacent about your markets. Make sure you not only recognize changes as they occur but also anticipate those changes to whatever extent possible. React to the changes before they cause sales and profit problems.

On a frequent basis ask yourself: What product, service, or other changes are my competitors introducing that could have an effect on my sales? What changes in the needs, demands, or buying decisions on the part of my customers might cause them to buy from my competitors? What technological changes might make my products obsolete? How are market prices likely to change over the next year and what can I do to address those changes? What are the market and business risks that could have a major adverse impact on my company?

Companies that don't change disappear. Those companies which continually react to market forces prosper. Make sure your company is in that second group.

Chapter 42 - Banking Relationships

Almost every company in the U.S. has a relationship with a commercial bank. In most cases, those banks are their primary source for working capital through a credit line and for investment capital through one or more term loans. Because of the importance of that relationship, you should carefully nurture your bank and the relationship between it and your company.

In general, your banker will be most comfortable if he or she knows what is happening with your company, good or bad. For that reason, you should send your financial statements to your bank representative no less than quarterly. Some loan documents, of course, require that you send those statements as often as monthly. In any case, the bank should have your financials in hand no more than twenty-one days after the close of the quarter or the month; fifteen days is even better.

You should then arrange to meet with your loan or bank officer about a week after he or she has received your company's financial information. During that meeting, you should review any significant changes in your company's financial results, discuss your projections as to future results or changes, and update the banker on any operational issues of importance.

In particular, if you will need additional funds within six months for a new piece of equipment, to finance an anticipated acquisition, or for any other reason, introduce the subject to your banker early. Having him or her participate in discussing and evaluating the use of those funds, the business risks associated with the new loan, and the anticipated results will contribute to the approval for the loan when the need is more immediate.

If your bank representative changes, ask the new person to visit your company, take them on a tour of your facilities, and introduce them to all key managers. Take a few minutes to carefully explain your company's business, markets, and competitive environment. Your banker can't understand your financial statements or react to additional loan requests unless he or she understands in what business you participate and how you approach your markets.

When there is any bad news, discuss it with your banker as soon as you recognize a problem, including, of course, your plans for addressing that problem. Bankers hate surprises. Also, if you only give your banker the good news, after a problem occurs, he or she will no longer have faith in what you tell them. Your banking relationship should at all times be open, frank, and factual.

If the bad news is really bad, your banking relationship may be transferred to the "special assets division". That is an euphemism for the "work-out" group. Hopefully, you will never meet a member of that group. If you do,

114

however, it is only because your bank believes there is a problem at your company so severe that the repayment of their loans is in doubt. In the work-out department, you'll meet a new type of banker. The friendship you might have enjoyed with your loan officer will be replaced by demands from a much less accommodating bank officer. You will be told to either solve the problem quickly or, more often, to find another banking relationship.

Of course, any problem severe enough to transfer your banking relationship to Special Assets should be one that you recognize and can address, if not cure, immediately. After all, if your loan repayment is in doubt, the entire future of your company is in doubt.

With those few clients of mine which have become candidates for Special Assets, we often when feasible replaced their bank with a less risk averse commercial lender. We also, however, quickly addressed the problems that caused the bank to question the repayment of their loan. Frequently, the resolution of the problem took longer than the banker's patience could stand, so replacing the banking relationship was an integral part of solving the problem.

In Chapter 36, I discussed the difference between banks and commercial lenders. As you might imagine, replacing one bank with another when a loan repayment is in doubt is particularly difficult. A commercial lender, however, will often lend funds to a company that would not be acceptable to a bank. In any case, not solving the problem or not replacing the original bank can result in your loan being deemed to be in default with all future payments accelerated by the bank. The result of that drastic action is most often a bankruptcy filing or company liquidation.

Your banking relationship and your attention to that relationship should help you avoid any of those draconian consequences of continuing losses or other corporate problems. I would imagine that you've often heard of using "OPM" or Other Peoples Money to sponsor or support corporate growth. Among the sources of OPM, your bank is most often the easiest to access. It is, therefore, particularly important that your company's relationship with its bank contribute to that access for both growth and operating capital.

Years ago, my father asked me, "If a banker has a glass eye, how can you tell which one it is? It's the one," he explained, "with that gleam of human kindness." That is rarely true but is more often true with the members of the Special Assets Division than with commercial loan officers.

Although you may have also heard that bankers will only lend money to those who don't need it, that is also a fabrication. However, your and your company's relationship with your bank will have an effect on its willingness to support the growth you need to prosper. Make sure that relationship is consistent with your need for those growth funds.

115

Chapter 43 - Delegation

At the inception of most companies, the founders have to handle the majority, if not all, of the management duties and often some of the production, service, or administrative duties as well. There is little need to delegate responsibilities to others as there are no others there to accept the assignments.

As companies grow, however, decisions must be made by the principal managers as to what duties to assign to others and what duties to keep themselves. Do it yourself or delegate. Those decisions can have a strong influence over the level of success your company can achieve. Even for larger, more mature companies, those decisions continue to be important.

In general, I favor a heavy dose of delegation. By giving added responsibilities and duties to those below you on the organization chart, you accomplish three specific goals:

(1) You have a better opportunity to assess the performance of your subordinates as they grapple with those new assignments;

(2) The delegation of those new tasks contributes to a broader range of experiences and, therefore, training for those subordinates;

(3) And you are grooming your successor, building management depth in the organization, and making the eventual choice of that successor an easier decision.

In addition, of course, you are also making your work load lighter and can then concentrate on those items of greatest importance. That doesn't mean that you can relax more but only that you can address those tasks that are better suited to your level of responsibility in the organization. You can't do it all. Why try?

Insufficient delegation can lead to a number of problems. Some years ago, I had a client who was the sole owner of a company with about $12 million in annual sales and a long history of profits. It was, however, a true one person company with a flat organization chart.

Almost everyone in the company reported to my client. Although I frequently suggested that he establish a more vertical organizational structure with many of his responsibilities delegated to others, he could not turn loose. He died suddenly. The worst possible choice for his successor then became president. Just over a year later, the company was no longer in existence.

116

Management succession, however, is not the only problem. I had another client with a horizontal organization. Without delegating much to her other managers, there was not enough time for my client to handle all of the various tasks and duties which she had assigned to herself. That company stagnated in a paralysis of unaddressed decisions and missed opportunities. It didn't grow and generated only anemic profits.

In addition to a lack of delegation, too much can also result in problems. Some years ago, I had a client who delegated virtually all decisions and responsibilities to others. With a void at the top, his company lacked both direction and controls. Various managers made decisions without regard to their effects on other departments. In addition, there was little, if any, attention to the results of those decisions.

One particularly inappropriate investment turned modest profits into losses in just a few months. With no centralized direction to address the losses, the company sank into a stagnant mess. Finally, the owner responded, took control, and corrected the problems.

In order to balance an appropriate amount of delegation between too little or too much, start by writing your own job description. List all of those items, functions, responsibilities, and decisions for which you are responsible. Then divide the list into those items which you absolutely can't appropriately delegate to others, those which you could delegate to others, and those which are a waste of your time and absolutely should be delegated to someone else.

Once that list is complete, then add a column to rank those items at which you excel, those for which your experience and talents are adequate, and those you do poorly. An analysis of that chart should help you determine if your delegating skills are sufficient and appropriate.

In addition, you should also draw an organization chart for your company or department (assuming your don't already have one, which you should). (Also see Chapter 29.) If more than six or seven people report to you, you may not be delegating enough of your responsibilities to others. How many people can you adequately supervise; how many problems can you discuss in a day; and how many decisions can and should you make?

Once you determine the level of delegation that is appropriate for you and your company or division, you've only completed half the exercise. You must also determine how to monitor the results produced by those to whom you delegated the various responsibilities. It is not good enough to simply say, "Here, you do this." You should then determine if the task was completed satisfactorily or if the responsibility was addressed appropriately. If it was, you may be able to delegate more to that person. If it was not, either you delegated to the wrong person or made a delegation decision that should be reversed.

Much of your success in your business activities will be determined by your ability to balance tasks, responsibilities, time allocation, and priorities without the comfort of many black or white, yes or no decisions. Business is not that simple. Making delegating decisions is one of those difficult areas where there are few rules. In addition, changing conditions, including corporate growth, may change what is the correct answer.

Consider whether there are enough hours in each day to accomplish what you should. Examine the extent to which you micro-manage your operations. Must you be involved in virtually every decision regardless of its importance? Do you find it difficult to relinquish a responsibility you've exercised over an extended period? Any of those are warning signs of an inability to delegate.

Consider whether you encounter too many surprises due to decisions made by others. Do you lack information about important corporate functions? Do you have periods of inactivity and feel that you aren't as involved as you should be? Any of those could be warning signs that you've delegated too much to others.

In a smooth running organization where you have time to concentrate on those items of greatest importance and sense when there are problems which need your attention, you've probably delegated just about the right amount of responsibility and authority to those reporting to you. Monitor that level of delegation periodically to determine if it remains appropriate to the growth, complexity, and environment in your company.

Chapter 44 - Code of Accounts

I would never recommend finding a comfortable chair, sitting down, and reading the white pages of the telephone book. There are, however, some business chores that approach the tedium of that exercise but are important nevertheless.

One of those is a periodic review and revision, or perhaps even a complete rewrite, of your company's code of accounts. That code is the DNA of your accounting software. It determines how your financial statements will be presented, what line items are shown, what sub-accounts are used to create those line items, and how much underlying detail is available for each revenue, expense, asset, and liability line on your financial statements.

Because concise, timely, and accurate financial statements should be one of your principal corporate control tools, how your financial statements are compiled and presented is of vital importance. Your code of accounts is the foundation for that presentation. The format for those codes is established by your accounting software. Usually the codes are four to eight or more digits which can be either all numerical or alpha/numeric. In any case, a single code is assigned to each accounting item you want to capture as a separate piece of financial information.

How the individual codes are handled, subtotaled, and totaled will also be established by your accounting software. Your software manual, another excruciatingly boring piece of reading, will determine how you compose the account codes to accumulate data that will total to a single line item on your statements. It will also tell you how to have a specific code become a line on your income statement or balance sheet. If your accounting software is adequate, it will also allow you to investigate any single line item, see the underlying codes and the related dollar amounts that total to that line, and continue to drill down to individual invoices or other revenue, expense, or additional accounting data.

Start a review of your code of accounts with a review of your monthly financial statements in their current format. You should look at each line item to determine whether it is important enough to be shown separately. As mentioned in Chapter 5, I've had clients managing companies with annual sales exceeding $20 million and found line items on their financial statements which totaled less than $100 per year. Those lines did not provide any valuable control information and should have been combined as one element of a more appropriate category or line item.

I've also had clients with fifty or more line items in their General & Administrative accounts but only a single line for revenues and another for direct cost or cost of goods sold. Ask yourself, which is more important to

119

track, understand, and control: the cost of postage or manufacturing labor and material costs. The answer should be obvious.

The first line or lines of your income statement show your company's revenue. Those revenue items should be divided into appropriate control categories with a single account code and line item for each. If, for instance, you produce or sell several different product categories, you should have a revenue line item for each. If you sell similar products into several different markets, you should have a revenue line for each of those markets. Determine what revenue categories you should track over time and make sure each has a separate account code and is shown as a separate line on your income statement.

Next, consider your direct cost or cost of goods sold. If your company is a manufacturer, those direct costs should include line items for production labor, raw material purchases, and factory overhead. If your company is only a distributor, your direct costs might include separate lines for each category of purchased goods for resale.

By the way, in regard to labor costs, either direct or G&A, I always like to show only a total that includes all payroll taxes, employee benefit costs, and workers' compensation premiums. Your primary concern should be the total cost of employing the staff necessary to perform each company function, not the amount of FUTA tax you incurred. If you need to study such underlying details, an appropriate code of accounts and accounting software should allow you to expand any labor cost line to show its individual components.

Of course, the difference between your total revenues and direct costs defines your company's gross profits, perhaps your most important single accounting item and the one that most closely relates to your company's ability to generate profits. A single revenue line and a single direct cost line are not sufficient to monitor, track, and control gross profits.

Some companies should have three direct cost line items, some should have six, and some should also capture various indirect production costs. You use your code of accounts to make those distinctions and format your financial statements for maximum utility.

In that regard, you should be careful to capture as individual line items only those G&A or operating expenses necessary for a summary presentation. For instance, I frequently recommend an "Occupancy Cost" line that includes facility rent, all utility expense, janitorial expense, landscaping costs, and property taxes. If you need to see those subcategories, your code of accounts and accounting software should allow you to expand the Occupancy Costs line to show those individual items.

Once you determine what line items on your income statement and balance sheet are important, you can then review your code of accounts, usually with your accounting manager, to determine how the individual codes should be structured to produce the statements that will give you the best control information. When establishing those individual codes, it's a good idea to leave plenty of unused numbers. Over time, you may find that you need to add a code to a subtotal or even add a line item to your financial statements. If an appropriate code number is not available, that can be a difficult task.

In addition, changing code numbers can also be difficult depending upon your accounting software and how it both formats and uses the code of accounts. For that reason, it's often best to review your code of accounts near the end of your fiscal year and make all changes on the first day of the new year.

In addition to formatting your financial statements for ease of review, tracking, and control, your code of accounts review will also tell you whether your accounting software is appropriate. Also, if that software will not show each line item as a percent of revenues, it is not adequate. Those percentages allow you to track changes in a way that looking only at dollar amounts cannot.

In any case, think about your financial statements and how they are used. Your code of accounts may need some adjustment.

Chapter 45 - Operate As If Your Company Is Publicly Owned

It is unlikely that the company you manage, or for which you manage a division or department, will ever be publicly owned or be a part of a public company. The great majority of companies in the U.S. are started and managed by entrepreneurs and remain owned by their founders until they are eventually sold to larger, but still privately owned, companies. That does not mean, however, that you can't learn valuable lessons from publicly owned companies. In that regard, I contend that most privately owned companies should be managed as if their common stock was listed on the NASDAQ market. (Also see Chapter 14.)

Start by treating your financial statements as if your company were publicly owned. Give copies to each member of your company's management group. Send copies each quarter or each month to your bank loan officer. If major suppliers or customers ask for copies of your financials, send them. (Also see Chapter 8.) If those financial results don't show strength, find out why and cure the problem. Hiding bad financial results is not a part of the solution to such problems.

Also, have your financial statements audited each year just like a publicly owned company is required to do. Certainly an audit cost more than a review or compilation, but that difference is an investment in future options. A CPA's audit letter is the "Good Housekeeping Seal of Approval" for your financials. With audited results, banks will be more accommodating. Should you ever want to sell common stock to the public or even in some private offerings, audited financials going back three years will be a requirement. And at any time that you decide to sell you company to a larger corporation, having audited financials will not only make the transaction easier but should also positively influence the purchase price.

In addition, as a part of many annual audits, most CPAs also include a "management letter". That is a letter to the management of the company which is not a part of the audit report. It explains problems with either financial reporting, internal controls, or operations, which the auditor found while performing the audit procedures. That letter from an unaffiliated, independent advisor is often alone worth the additional cost for the audit. The higher cost for an audit should be a particularly attractive investment in the future for both your company and its management group.

All publicly owned companies are required to have outside or unaffiliated directors on their Boards. You should also copy that practice. (Also see

122

Chapter 16.) Too many small companies have only their owners as directors and meet only once a year, if that often. But what can you learn talking with yourself? Expand your Board of Directors to include business people who are not employees. First, that is a wonderful way of getting good advice for free or for the $500 per meeting fees you might pay your outside directors. It also introduces a valuable discipline related to the preparation of your quarterly meetings. You will be forced to review your operations each quarter and explain your results to outsiders.

Most business people have now heard many of the stories about the cost of Sarbanes-Oxley compliance for publicly owned companies. That legislation is formally titled the "Public Company Accounting Reform and Investor Protection Act of 2002". Although I don't suggest that you comply with every aspect of that complex law, its primary objective is to assure that a public company's financial reporting is accurate and that fraud and other nefarious activities are, to the extent possible, eliminated. That is not a bad objective for all companies.

As a part of your annual audit, you should ask your CPA to examine your internal control procedures, your possible exposure to financial fraud, and other matters that relate to your operations which might expose your company to sudden losses or other problems. You won't need all of the Sarbanes-Oxley compliance requirements, but some element of those examinations and controls may not only be valuable but might also prevent unpleasant surprises in the future.

Another good practice you might adopt from larger and generally publicly owned companies is a set of comprehensive written operating procedures. Those might not only contribute to your ability to manage individual operating functions but may also prevent litigation related to, for instance, your hiring and employee termination methods. Although your company's managers know how to do what they've done for years, you might be surprised to find problems and omissions when you attempt to write those procedures into an operating manual. By delegating the development of various sections of the written procedures to your managers responsible for individual functions, you will also learn more about their approach to their jobs. (Also see Chapter 59.)

And finally, don't steal from yourself. Many small companies reward their owners and some key managers with perquisites that aren't available or appropriate in a public company environment. Guess what? Many of those aren't appropriate for any company, public or private. In addition to the elimination of potential tax problems, if you ever expect to sell your company, you will never receive full credit for hidden expenses which were a part of your owners' or executives' compensation. If any personal expenses charged to your company would not pass IRS scrutiny, drop them. Paying taxes is a high class problem; tax fraud is a problem of another magnitude. (Also see Chapter 35.)

Your company may never be publicly owned; it may never reach near the size that would be required for an initial public offering. However, if you pattern your operations around those required of a public company, you'll never regret having that level of operating discipline and controls. In addition, at some point, your company might qualify to raise funds in an IPO, or you may want to sell your company to a publicly owned corporation. By operating now as if your company were public, all of those options will be available. Without ever exercising any of those options, however, you can assure that your company will be better managed and will have controls in place to help assure continued growth and profits.

124

Chapter 46 - Most Valuable Assets

I buy and sell companies for my clients. On either side of such a transaction, much attention is paid to the various assets of the company being bought or sold. Most of that attention, however, is directed toward the tangible rather than intangible assets, those items which can be touched. Although those tangible assets might be easier to value, they are not always the most valuable nor the most important of a company's assets. Instead, I would contend that the three most valuable assets of any company are rarely discussed as a part of an acquisition or sale transaction. Those three assets are people, money, and your own time.

In the case of a pure service company, people are the company. Even for a manufacturing operation, its employees make it function. Without them, the company has no value other than what might be received in a liquidation of its equipment, inventory, and accounts receivable. During most of his career, my father managed a major engineering construction firm. He frequently said that one hundred percent of his inventory got on the elevator every evening and went home. A major portion of his job was to assure that they would return the next morning.

If you clearly recognize the value of the people who give your company the ability to generate its revenues, profits, and enterprise value, you will recognize how important it is to assure that your company is their employer of choice. Treat every member of your entire corporate team as if your success and the success of your company depended on them, because, in fact, it does. In that regard, I am a great fan of incentive compensation. If your company prospers, make sure those who create that prosperity participate in it. Otherwise, why should they do an exceptional rather than an acceptable job? (Also see Chapter 22.)

As to that second most valuable asset, years ago, my father also told me, "Money is like blood. When it stops flowing, you're dead." He was right. Guard your capital resources as if your company's existence depended upon them; it does.

There are a number of important aspects to money management. You should pay attention to them all. Every month your comptroller should compute your average accounts receivable collection period or days in receivables. If that collection period lengthens, you're investing cash in your accounts receivable, and that cash is not available to support your daily operations. Keeping accounts receivable collections current also reduces bad debt losses.

125

Inventory turns are also important. If you devote cash to an increase in inventory, that cash will also be unavailable until the inventory is sold. If you can increase your inventory turns or reduce that level of inventory needed to support your revenues, the savings will equal the interest on the funds you don't need to borrow for an investment in additional inventory.

As another part of cash management, calculate your working capital levels every month. That is: current assets minus current liabilities. The amount of working capital available to your company is a measure of its ability to pay its short-term operating obligations as they come due. Over time, you can compute the level of working capital needed to maintain those operations at various revenue levels. Then as your company grows, you can plan for its future working capital needs and determine what portion of those should come from earnings and what portion from borrowed funds.

You should also know what level of cash is needed to support your operations. In some cases, this may actually be zero. For instance, if you use a bank credit line as a part of your working capital, arrange with your bank to set up a "sweep account" which maintains your cash balance at zero and your credit line balance at a low level. The interest savings will be a direct contribution to profits.

You should also have your comptroller create a cash flow analysis each month in addition to your income statement and balance sheet. That cash flow statement will show you what investments you are making in each aspect of your company's operations. You can then use that statement to track trends over time and better manage your use and availability of cash reserves.

In regard to your own time as one of your company's principal assets, control its application just as you do your company's cash. Learn to delegate and to allocate your time to those tasks for which your experience and talents are best suited. (Also see Chapter 43.) Make sure that the limited hours you have to devote to the prosperity of your business are channeled in the best direction. You can't do it all, so you should concentrate your efforts on those items most directly related to the growth, profits, and financial strength of your company.

While I'm on the subject, I should also mention the fourth most valuable corporate asset. It's your company's market position. It's not its manufacturing capability. It's not its products or services, and it's not its suppliers. If you can control a segment of your market, you can have your products manufacturer by others. You can also substitute or add other products or services which your customer base can use. You can find new suppliers, but creating a market segment that you can control and, perhaps, even dominate is difficult and both cost and time consuming.

Calculate the percent of your current sales which is generated by your past customers. That's the market you can and should control. Guard those

126

customers with care, and make sure they remain your customers. As a result, your company will prosper.

Think about your company's most valuable assets and make sure you protect those above all else. If you can do that, the value of those assets will continue to increase for you and for all others associated with your company and its operations.

127

Is This Any Way to Run a Company?   H. Lee Rust

Chapter 47 - Risk Management

In Chapter 15, we talked about corporate waste and areas where you might reduce expenses. In this chapter, I would like to look at another of those areas where expense should be carefully controlled: risk management and its related business insurance, safety programs, and workers' compensation coverage. Too few companies regularly assess their exposure to these risks and their costs or understand the direct expense associated with, for instance, a lax safety environment.

Among your corporate advisors, in addition to your accountant and attorney, every company should have an experienced and highly qualified insurance agent. Once each year, that agent should consult with you on your insurance in force, make suggestions as to coverage you don't have but might consider, and assure that the insurance you have is low cost but is placed with financially strong underwriters. Your agent should also make suggestions as to the elimination of coverage you have which might not be cost effective for your company.

If you don't have an agent who understands your business, interview several just as you would any other corporate advisor. Then chose an agent who specializes in business coverage, carries multiple lines, represents a variety of indemnity companies, and will work hard for you and your company.

Insurance coverage is a significant expense item. It should not be a source of corporate waste. There are insurance policies for every imaginable contingency. Some are absolutely necessary; others should be considered optional depending upon the situation in your company and an assessment of your realistic business risks.

For every acquisition I arrange for my clients, I always include the client's insurance agent as a part of the due diligence team. It's the responsibility of that agent to review the acquisition target's insurance coverage and to determine how, and on what schedule, that coverage can be combined with the parent company's policies. There should be some savings in that consolidation of coverage. Of course, the agent must also determine that the target company's coverage is not only adequate but also in force as of the closing date.

In regard to insurance coverage, we all understand the high cost of employee health coverage. That is another area where the advice of an expert can be of great value. In addition to considerations of how much coverage to offer your employees and how to divide the premium costs with them, your

128

agent might also advise you on a high deductible policy with self-insurance up to the deductible amount. That is a form of stop-loss policy that could result in significant savings. It does, however, usually require that your company provide the administrative services for those health-related payments under the deductible ceiling.

Many companies provide their employee health insurance through the use of a Professional Employer Organization, often referred to as an employee leasing company. Those PEOs can often provide good health coverage at lower cost because they can consolidate that coverage among a large number of their client companies. The savings in health insurance cost usually exceeds the other costs associated with using the PEO for all payroll and other employee compensation functions.

Although you might not be able to control the steadily increasing costs of employee benefit insurance, you can usually control another insurance expense which for many companies is the most costly of all their coverage: workers' compensation insurance. The cost of that state mandated coverage is directly related to your company's safety record. Certainly, a single employee can have a major accident which adversely effects your experience rating, but that does not excuse a lack of attention to employee safety. Regular safety training for your employees can result in workers' comp savings that more than compensate for the time spent in the training sessions.

In addition, you should assure that your employees are exposed to the minimum safety risks possible. I'm sure you've been in factories where the safety record, "___ accident free days", is posted on a large sign. That is only one example of an emphasis on safe practices. In the previous chapter, I said that your employees are among the three most valuable of your company's assets. Poor safety dissipates the value of that asset.

Many companies, some of even modest size, have a full-time Risk Manager. That member of the executive team should be a one person profit center. Your Risk Manager should save substantially in excess of his or her compensation each year by assuring that your business insurance is appropriate, that your company is following well defined hiring and termination practices, and that your safety program is an active one, among other duties.

In addition to written hiring and termination policies, a company's Risk Manager often maintains the employee files, assures that performance reviews are conducted regularly, and that appropriate reports are kept in each person's employment file. The Risk Manager might also be responsible for developing and maintaining a written Policy and Procedure Manual that relates to employee practices as well as other administrative procedures. (Also see Chapter 59.)

By the way, limiting litigation risks is also a part of risk management, particularly in today's litigation prone business environment. The assessment of litigation risks should usually be a joint effort on the part of a company's Risk Manager and other appropriate members of its executive team together with its independent CPA firm and its corporate attorney. No less than once each year, your company's litigation risks should be discussed with those advisors. You can't completely avoid the possibility of costly litigation, but you can minimize that risk and also build defenses into your company's risk management program.

No company is risk free, but you can control or minimize your corporate exposure to unforeseen costs that have little relationship to your revenues and normal business activities. Provide your employees with a safe working environment, make sure you have adequate but not excessive insurance coverage, and regularly assess your company's exposure to a law suit from a customer, supplier, competitor, or employee.

If an employee is in a hospital, he or she can't do their job. If you are testifying in court, you can't do yours. Work as hard to eliminate those risks as you do producing the goods or services your company sells.

Chapter 48 - Equity Financing

In Chapter 36, we talked about debt financing and, in regard to other capital sources, mentioned the sale of equity or common stock. Let's now look at that capital source. In general, the sale of common stock or any other form of equity securities in a closely held private company is much more difficult than arranging a loan from a bank or commercial lender. Of course, if a bank or commercial lender won't extend their credit to a company, their reasons for that reticence will also be reasons for an equity investor to be cautious.

Selling common stock often seems so easy and attractive. Just sell a minority participation in your company to an investor, and use the funds to support future growth. As the company grows, there is no need to pay the equity investor any interest or a return of principal. The investor will only participate in a future liquidating event, i.e. a sale of the company or an initial public offering (IPO) it might arrange.

From the investor's point of view, however, that minority participation can be a high risk use of funds with no guarantee of ever receiving any return and with the possibility of losing their entire investment. Years ago my father asked me the value of a minority ownership position in a closely held company. When I said I didn't know because I didn't know anything about the company, he explained that it was zero. "It doesn't," he said, "pay any dividends, doesn't necessarily provide any gainful employment, and usually can't be sold." Such an equity participation has value only when a liquidating event occurs, and there can be no assurance of that ever occurring.

Although I've been successful over the past several decades in raising equity funds for a limited number of my clients, I take a somewhat jaundiced view of that capital source. Without trying to be overly negative, my views of the major sources for equity investments are:

Institutional Venture Capital Firms (including Private Equity Funds) - These equity investors generally target their funds toward high technology, medical, or other companies with a high proprietary component to their operations and a high probability of either selling the company to a much larger corporation at a high multiple of future earnings or "going public". The attention span for these venture investors is usually five years or less. Only a minuscule percentage of companies can match the investment requirements set by the majority of, if not all, venture capital and private equity firms. Those often include annual EBITDA (Earnings Before Interest, Taxes, Depreciation, and Amortization) generation in excess of $1 or $2 million.

131

"Angels" - These are high net worth individuals who write big checks for minority positions in high risk ventures. For the past thirty-five years, I've heard about such investors but never met one. Angel investors usually put their funds in markets they understand well from previous jobs or ventures or, on occasion, join investment groups which then resemble venture capital firms. Finding an appropriate angel investor and then convincing him or her to actually make an investment in your company can vary from highly speculative to impossible.

Corporate Investors - These are companies which, in general, participate in the same or a similar market as the firm needing growth capital. In addition, corporate investors must have a reason to support the success of the smaller operation. This is the equity market in which my clients and I have had the most success raising capital funds. Appropriate corporate investors might include one of your suppliers, a large customer, or a market related company that may want to acquire your company after its success has been proven.

Individual Investors - These are not angels but are people of more limited means who may want to support your corporate efforts simply because they know you and have faith in your ability to build a company. Although my clients and I have also had some success tapping this source of equity funds, the available dollars are usually limited.

If an appropriate and interested equity investor for your company can be located, pricing a minority participation can also be difficult. Because that price is almost always based on projections of future revenues and profits, the price per share or price per percent ownership today cannot be calculated with any assurance as to its accuracy or whether it is or is not appropriate. Also, because most company owners have an inflated idea as to the value of their company as well as its future potential, their idea of a fair price may be significantly higher than what an investor will pay.

To resolve such a pricing question, I usually use a relatively simple method of calculating equity values. First, I generate a five year income statement and balance sheet projection. I then apply a reasonable multiple to the fifth year EBITDA and subtract projected levels of interest bearing debts to calculate the anticipated value for the entire company in five years. (Also see Chapter 21.)

I then take the investment unit, say $100,000, and multiply it by five; that is, an investment return of five times the funds at risk over a five year period. That $500,000 future value requirement divided by the total projected value for the entire company will be the percent ownership the investor must have today in order to achieve the expected return of five times the funds at risk in five years.

Too often, that calculation shows that the company's owners would have to relinquish a much greater percentage of their equity than is palatable. It is,

132

however, an exercise that presents a company's owners with a realistic method of calculating the current value of their company's future potential.

Another particularly complex element in the sale of common stock or other equity securities in a privately held company is compliance with the Securities and Exchange Commission (SEC) regulations for the sale of securities in a private offering. In general, equity sales to institutional or corporate investors will be exempt from most of those rules. Sales to individuals, however, must follow specific SEC rules as to disclosure requirements, the number of investors to whom the offer is made, and the methods used to make those offers, among other both SEC and state mandated requirements.

This is an area of securities law that requires the careful attention of an experienced securities attorney. Although I've drafted many private offering documents (and several IPO registration statements), I would never present such an offering to anyone other than an exempt investor without the review and advice of a securities attorney.

Is the sale of an ownership interest in a small company an attractive source of growth capital? Absolutely. Can it be done? Sometimes, but always with significant difficulty. Before you embark on such a capital raising effort, assess the sources for those funds as well as your probability of success in attracting the needed funds from those sources. (Also see Chapter 32.) If either your potential capital sources or their ability or willingness to invest is in doubt, look for other ways to support your company's growth.

133

Chapter 49 - Corporate Character

B ack in 1969, I cut a cartoon out of The Wall Street Journal which showed an executive saying to his stockholders, "And though in 1969, as in previous years, your company had to contend with spiraling labor costs, exorbitant interest rates, and unconscionable government interference, management was able once more, through a combination of deceptive marketing practices, false advertising, and price fixing, to show a profit which, in all modesty, can only be called excessive."

That cartoon depicted a company with problems of the Enron kind. It reminded me of my father saying that companies take on individual character traits just as people do and that those corporate characteristics are a reflection of the company's key executives. He explained that a company headed by an arrogant dictator would not be a comfortable environment for a manager who did not share that management style. Neither would a company with an particularly personable president be a compatible place for an arrogant dictator. As a result, most of the management staff at most companies or in most departments tend to mirror the characteristics of the boss. Over time, the company itself takes on that character.

We now know that Enron was managed by a group who believed they were better than others and could, therefore, make decisions that evolved from ill advised to fraudulent. The erosion of the Enron corporate character destroyed one of the then largest companies in the U.S.

The lesson here is that you can influence and mold the character of your company and how it is viewed by others. That character can then, in turn, have a significant impact on the success of your company in its markets. (Also see Chapter 33.)

Start by considering the character of the individual members of your company's management team and how those character traits match the way you would like the company to be perceived by others. Then define those corporate characteristics which should be important to you, to your company, and to its various constituents. Make sure that every member of your company's management team understands those characteristics and why you feel they are important.

When hiring new management personnel, be sure to explain how you want the outside world to think about your company and its character. Then make sure any new hire matches that character as closely as you can.

Not long ago, I had a client company in the construction subcontracting business, one with high employee turnover and low levels of corporate loyalty.

134

As a result, it had chronic problems staffing its growth, particularly during periods of high activity. To cure that problem, the management of that company decided to make it the employer of choice in its market area.

They started apprentice training and craft accreditation programs for its project workers. They also instituted a program of project specific bonuses for all field employees who worked on jobs which exceeded stated profit levels. They added an employee newsletter to the company's website and made sure all the field workers knew it was there. And they asked various company employees on a regular basis about their work environment and how it might be improved.

That company's reputation with trades craftsmen in its market area improved, and it did become known as the employer of choice. It paid higher wages, including those bonuses, but both project execution and profits improved. Staffing projects became a larger problem for its competitors than for it, and its ability to staff those projects became one of its competitive advantages.

Contrast that with the recurring magazine and newspaper articles describing Wal-Mart as a company which built its low price strategy by treating its employees and suppliers with distain. Now that perception of Wal-Mart's character has spawned boycotts, high employee turnover, increased union organizing activity, and government scrutiny. I wonder what Sam Walton would think.

You might remember him as the man who built the world's largest retail chain by buying, wherever possible, American made goods, serving the rural areas shunned by the K-Marts, and providing a fair wage for a day's work. Since Sam's time, the character of Wal-Mart has changed for the worst. Can the company be better served by that change?

Periodically, you should attempt to assess your company's character and the effect of that corporate character on its operations and financial results. Survey some of your customers to ask specifically how they perceive your company's character. You might want to use an outside consultant to conduct such a survey once every year or two. Use a similar survey technique with your suppliers. In addition, ask your employees to complete a questionnaire that focuses on their perception of your company as a place to work as well as its reputation in its markets.

Compile the results of all those surveys into a description of your company's corporate character. Then look at what changes you might want to make in that perception of character. If the members of your company's management team understand the importance of that perception by all of their constituents, they can work together to change it.

I had another client company which had what I would call an aloof character. Its management team simply wasn't completely cognizant of how

135

their company was perceived and didn't seem to care. That company finally succumbed to its apathy and was bought by one which was better perceived in its markets.

You can not only influence your company's character, you can chose what it should be and then achieve that choice. The results should be attractive for your company, its customers, its employees, its suppliers, and its owners.

Chapter 50 - Technology Upgrades

In regard to the two brick manufacturing plants mentioned in Chapter 18, over the years, an interesting contrast developed between the two. Initially, starting in the 1930's, both plants cured their bricks in "beehive" kilns. The soft clay extrusions had to be hand stacked in each of the round kilns, fired, and then removed by hand. In the mid-1950's, the plant in Virginia was rebuilt with the addition of a continuous tunnel kiln. The majority owners of the Alabama plant said they couldn't justify that exorbitant expense.

When I managed the Virginia plant from 1971 through 1975, we again updated all the equipment, adding fans to lower the time in the drying chamber and installing the newest impingement gas jet burners to improve the firing characteristics and increase the speed through the kiln. The Alabama plant was still hand stacking brick in their old beehive kilns, about the same way it was done two centuries before. Profits had dropped to almost zero. Some years ago, the Virginia plant was sold at a nice premium to a larger construction products company and is still operating. At about the same time, the Alabama plant was closed following a number of years of losses.

The experience of those two companies is a lesson in technology upgrades. If your company manufactures, fabricates, or assembles a product, adding newer technology is often not a question of whether you can afford it but whether you can afford not to have it. Even if you're in a pure service business, the addition of newer technology used in delivering those services can be extremely important.

One of my clients is a metal fabrication job shop. That's an almost ruinously competitive business. My client often says he has to compete with any welder who has a cutting torch and a welding machine in the back of a pickup truck. His method of separating his services from the large number of competing metal working shops in his market area is to buy the latest production equipment. Those almost continuous technology upgrades give him three competitive advantages.

The first is lower fabrication costs. By having highly automated equipment, my client can produce more with fewer labor hours. His second competitive advantage is a combination of capacity and speed. His investments in equipment allow him to lower his production cycle and, therefore, increase the capacity of his plant without adding either space or people. And third, by using his relatively high technology equipment, he can bid on projects for which smaller, less technologically advanced competitors can't match the exacting specifications. The gross profit margins for this job shop are significantly higher than those of its competitors.

In regard to a service company, in the 1950's, my father invested over a million dollars in a computer for his engineering operation. That computer, by the way, was probably not as powerful as your cell phone is today. When I asked him what that computer could do for his company, he said he didn't know. He went on to explain, however, that much of engineering was based on complex formulas and calculations. He believed that his managers and engineers could learn how to use the computer, find out what it could do, and gain some competitive advantage.

That engineering company was one of the first to use computer aided, critical path scheduling techniques, to write software to calculate steel structure loading parameters, and to adopt CAD (computer aided design) drawing techniques. It was a particularly successful and highly profitable company which was then sold to a major conglomerate in 1969.

There are two principal methods of evaluating technology upgrades or the related purchase of new equipment. The first is a relatively simple cost/benefit analysis. Analyze and calculate the cost savings the equipment might provide. Those savings could be in lower labor hours, higher production volumes, less down time, lower warranty expense, or a reduction in scrap. Consider and quantify each element of lower costs as well as any additional expenses that might be associated with the purchase of the new technology.

One of those added costs is the interest expense associated with the purchase, including imputed interest on the capital cost even if no borrowed funds are needed. Other added costs might include higher utility usage, additional repair and maintenance expense, or training expense for the equipment operators.

Once you've projected the total savings less the additional cost of ownership, you can then compute the payback period. That period is the time required to fully amortize the capital cost of the equipment from the net savings it will generate. If that payback period is four years or less, there should be little question regarding the purchase of the newer technology. If the payback period is more than four years, you then need to examine the second method of evaluating the technology upgrade.

That is an analysis of what changes will occur in the competitive environment if your competitors install the latest technology and you don't. Although the payback period may be longer than you would like, if the technology investment would give your competitors a distinct advantage, your potential loss of revenues and related profits is a cost of not buying the equipment. That's what happened to the Alabama brick plant that couldn't afford to buy the tunnel kiln. In fact, they couldn't afford not to; they just didn't know that at the time.

Another important element for evaluating technology upgrades is your company's ability to finance the equipment costs. For discussing such

138

equipment financing with your bank, commercial lenders, equipment leasing companies, or the equipment supplier, your cost/benefit analysis will be of great help. If you can clearly show that the savings from the new equipment will fully amortize its costs in less than the five years, which is usually the maximum term for an equipment loan, financing the purchase should not be difficult. In addition, don't neglect to consider both equipment leasing companies and financing that might be offered by the equipment supplier. Both of those capital sources will frequently finance an equipment purchase that your bank might not.

Regardless of the type of company or division of that company you might manage, continually evaluate the newest technology you could use to lower your costs, increase your capacity, or otherwise improve your competitive position. Give your production team the most efficient tools available and then monitor the effects of having those tools on your company's financial results.

Another of my clients provides gas leak detection surveys for utilities. They were the first in their industry to mount their detection equipment on the Segway Human Transporter. The resulting increase in detection speeds gave that company a distinct competitive advantage. That company also developed what is still the only laser based gas detector incorporating improvements in safety, detection speed, and accuracy. Gas leak detection is a mundane business. The technology employed by my client in that business is not at all mundane. That company, by the way, is now the largest in its industry.

139

Chapter 51 - IP Protection

M ost people believe that a patent will protect an invention or proprietary item from being copied. It won't. A patent simply gives the patent holder the right to sue anyone who copies the patented device. That means that the patent holder must have the resources needed to file suit, pursue their rights in court, and win what is often a highly technical and complex legal battle.

Meanwhile, filing the patent gives potential competitors a detailed description, together with the design and specifications, for the patented device. Using that material, those competitors can attempt to copy the item, perhaps with enough change to avoid patent infringement or perhaps as only a simple copy with no regard to the patent.

Some years ago, I had a client whose company was in the business of developing and selling highly technical communications interface equipment. The company patented those devices and then had most of them manufactured in Asia. They found, however, that their suppliers were copying the equipment and, with some minor attempts at subterfuge, selling it in direct competition with my client's company. That company couldn't compete with its suppliers and did not have the resources to support protracted litigation on an international scale. After several years of battling that competition, my client's company was finally sold to one of its suppliers which was also one of those competitors.

This does not mean, of course, that you should not patent proprietary designs, only that you should be realistic about the extent of that protection. You should also use additional methods to protect your company's intellectual property. For many companies, their intangible assets, including such items as the design of patented devices, proprietary manufacturing methods, customer lists, and corporate names and logos, among many others, are a significant part of their enterprise value. Those items of intellectual property may also be major contributors to the companies' ability to generate their revenues and profits.

All of those intangible assets and intellectual properties should be carefully protected. Filing for a patent is only one element of that protection.

If your company develops or produces patentable items, you should have a patent attorney on retainer. That attorney can give you advice as to which items should be patented. He or she can also help you develop other methods of protecting your intellectual property and can give you advice to prevent your infringing on a patent held by another company.

One method of protecting many written and visual materials, including corporate or product names, marketing materials, logos, and some computer data, is the use of copyrights. Even "trade dress" or the colors and layout of your product labels or other identification can be the subject of a copyright. Again, your patent attorney should be helpful in developing guidelines as to what materials should be protected and assisting you in establishing simple procedures for securing copyrights.

In addition, all companies should have a well crafted confidentiality, noncompetition, and non-solicitation agreement which should be signed by any outside party who might have access to the company's intellectual property. The confidentiality segment defines those materials and binds the party to maintain their confidential nature. The noncompetition agreement prevents the unaffiliated party from using the confidential material in competition with your company. And the non-solicitation segment prevents such an outside party from hiring your employees and, in some instances, soliciting your customers. Such an agreement or agreements will usually include an "injunctive relief" provision that would allow you to have a court, at minimal costs, quickly issue an injunction against a continuing violation of the agreement.

Another consideration for the protection of intellectual property or intangible assets is an employee confidentiality and noncompetition agreement. Those should also include non-solicitation provisions related to both hiring your company's employees and soliciting its customers. Few companies use noncompetition agreements, but many should. Such an agreement can't be so broad as to prevent your company's employees from having gainful employment at another company but, within narrow parameters, can offer significant protection against one of your company's employees using the training and experiences its provided to compete in its markets.

Certainly all salespeople should sign confidentiality and customer non-solicitation agreements, if not complete noncompetition agreements. Similar agreements should also be signed by all officers, directors, and key management personnel. In fact, it's usually a good idea to have the execution of such an agreement as a standard part of hiring any employee. If a new hire has a problem with a reasonably narrow confidentiality, noncompetition, and non-solicitation agreement, it's best that you find out why before such a person is given access to your company's intellectual property.

You've worked hard to develop the competitive advantages that contribute to your company's success and its future. Protect all of those advantages which are a part of your company's intellectual property using, where appropriate, patents and copyrights as well as confidentiality, noncompete, and non-solicitation agreements. Devote simple but prudent attention to the

141

proprietary nature of those assets. You certainly protect your company's cash; use the same extent of protection for those assets which generate that cash.

Chapter 52 - Don't Fall in Love

W hen I either buy or sell companies for my clients, I frequently tell them, "Don't fall in love with the deal", or put another way, "Breaking up is hard to do." After all the time, effort, and expense devoted to an acquisition or to the sale of a company, when warning signs appear, particularly late in the transaction, they can be inordinately difficult to properly assess. It's even harder to accept that the warnings may mean the deal should be abandoned. It's too easy to rationalize that a problem can be cured after the closing, but if it can't, your company has bought additional problems rather than solutions and probably overpaid for them.

In the case of a company sale, I've represented business owners who terminated an otherwise attractive transaction because of a clash of cultures between his or her company and those of the buyer. Although the sellers might have taken their money and retired, they wanted the sale to represent an increased opportunity for the numerous employees who had contributed to the value of their company. When they felt it would not, they turned to another potential buyer, even at a somewhat lower price.

This same principal applies to other aspects of business and to your company's operations. When asked why some procedure is followed, the answer should never include, "Because we've always done it that way." The only appropriate answer is, "We studied the issue and felt this procedure was the best method we could afford."

Don't fall in love with any aspect of how your company is managed, operated, or functions. In fact, a good practice is to question everything. I'm not suggesting that you also change everything and continually disrupt your operations with those changes, but do study alternate methods, sources, and procedures. When one of those is clearly better than what you've done in the past, adopt the new idea. (Also see Chapter 50.)

I had a client some time ago who wanted a second warehouse and distribution point separate from his manufacturing facility. He had his accountant produce an economic analysis for the new facility, comparing its cost to the anticipated freight savings. That analysis showed that the remote warehouse could not be justified.

Rather than abandon the idea, my client simply changed the criteria until the savings were greater than the additional cost. That remote facility almost cost him his entire company. Happily, the warehouse turned out to be a fair real estate investment which almost, but not quite, offset the operating losses when the building was finally sold. The disruption, caused first by the move into the remote warehouse and then by the move out, however, had a substantial negative effect on the other operations which lasted for months on both ends of that transaction.

It's easy to deal with a supplier you know and have bought from for years, but are that supplier's prices and terms the best you can do? A number of my clients who have a few major suppliers have adopted a set procedure of soliciting competitive bids for their components on no less than an annual basis. By buying with an annual contract, the company realizes the pricing and other benefits of large volume purchases and consistent orders. In addition, each supplier knows they will have to re-bid at the end of that one year contract and that their past performance will be a part of the evaluation process. If you've long purchased the same item from the same supplier, ask yourself, "Is that supplier the best I can find?" Don't fall in love with the deal nor with other companies from which you purchase either materials or services.

And if your company manufacturers a product, you should continually ask the "make or buy" question. In that regard, I frequently suggest to my manufacturing clients that they think of their company as being market rather than manufacturing driven. If by buying from another supplier, either components or entire assemblies, you can improve the quality of your product and lower its cost, ask yourself why you manufacture that item when you can buy it better and cheaper. (Also see Chapters 9 and 58.)

On several occasions over the years, I've had client companies which started out principally as manufacturing operations but slowly outsourced components until they converted their manufacturing space into an assembly, testing, and finished goods warehouse. They didn't fall in love with their manufacturing operations; they fell in love with their product and their ability to sell it at a competitive price that generated a high gross profit.

In Chapter 7, I addressed the "Peter Principal". That theory which states that an employee may be continually promoted until they reach their level of incompetence is a corollary to don't fall in love with the deal. If an employee has been placed in a position inappropriate to their skills, experience, or ability, they should be reassigned to a position better suited to them. The employee will be happier, and your company will run smoother.

The solution to our natural tendency to "fall in love with the deal" is to continually question the deal whether it is a major acquisition, an operating procedure, a make or buy decision for a minor part, or an employee who is not suited for their current position. Don't let lethargy become endemic simply because its easiest to do something the way its always been done. Find the best way and adopt that.

143

Chapter 53 - Sales Representatives

M any business managers, even some sales managers, believe that hiring a number of independent sales representatives will result in increased revenues. It won't. Certainly, such sales reps can provide an extent of geographic coverage that many companies might not be able to develop on their own. Rep organizations can also put more salespeople in the field than your company may be able to afford as salaried employees. Independent sales representatives (also called manufacturers representatives) provide a valuable service for companies all over the U.S., and you only pay commissions when they generate a sale.

However, the care and feeding of independent sales reps is of utmost importance. Done properly, it's time consuming and can be an expensive addition to the commissions you pay, although not as expensive as an in-house sales force of the same size. (Also see Chapter 6.)

Independent sales reps usually carry a number of related product lines. Your company's sales manager's job is not only to choose sales reps appropriate to your products or services but to then have them do more than just take sporadic orders. To be effective, your sales reps must actively present, promote, and sell your products and services in appropriate markets. They won't do that without consistent attention, training, and oversight.

As with many searches in today's world, a good place to start your rep search is the internet. A search for "Sales Representatives" quickly turns up Replocate.com, Rephunter.net, Globalrepresenation.com, and Gotsales.com. All of those websites advertise services to match sales reps to suppliers.

There are also a number of state specific sites that list sales reps in their area, as well as several sites which provide sales rep agreement forms. Another good source for reps might be suppliers of products complimentary, but not competitive, to yours. If they use sales reps, they should know which are the most effective. You might also call companies to whom you do or should sell your products and ask their purchasing manager what reps that call on them are the most effective.

In talking, initially by phone, with a potential sales rep firm or individual, determine what products or services they carry, to what companies they sell those products, how many individual salespeople they have on the road, their geographic coverage, the number of years they've been in business, and their website address. That information will give you a good preliminary idea as to whether that rep or firm is appropriate for your company. Obviously, you shouldn't engage reps who carry lines that compete with yours. Although

144

complementary products can be an asset, you also want to make sure the reps don't carry so many products that they can't devote much time to yours.

Although you can do a lot of your initial search work on the internet and by phone, prior to making a final choice about any rep firm or individual, a personal meeting is needed. With that, the costs of forming and managing a sales representative organization begins. For the initial meeting, it's best that you visit the rep or rep firm at their office. In addition to assessing the individuals' salesmanship, you'll also have an opportunity to see how well they manage their operations and how they will present themselves to your customers. After all, the reps' first sales job is to sell you on placing your lines with them.

Once a sales representative has been engaged, he or she must be trained. If this involves one person or a reasonably small group, you should invite them, at your expense, of course, to visit your facilities. They must not only understand your products and services, they must also be excited about selling your lines. That excitement is easier to promote if the sales reps have seen your operation, met your key people, and had an opportunity to see how your products are manufactured or sourced.

During that visit, you can also begin the sales rep training. This will include a thorough understanding of your various products and services, the competitive advantages and disadvantages of each, how those products and services are priced, and other information such as order to delivery times, special order handling, and your terms of sale.

After that, you must still provide periodic training for both new employees of the rep firm and refresher courses for the ones you trained previously. In addition, your company's sales manager or other appropriate member of its management group should arrange to make one or two days of sales calls with each of your sales reps at least twice a year and more frequently if the number of reps and your staffing permits.

Those joint calls give your reps an opportunity to see how you or your other managers sell your products and services. By having your sales rep schedule the joint calls well in advance, you'll also gain some insight into the number of calls the rep can make in a day, what companies they are seeing, and how they are received by the buyers in those companies.

By the way, as mentioned previously, the companies which are most effective in their use of sales representatives demand written sales call reports on no less than a weekly basis. These don't need to be lengthy or time consuming, but you need to know what sales calls your reps are making, their closing ratios, and summaries of the resistance they find to the purchase of your products and services.

145

The necessity of completing and sending those call reports will also keep your products and services consistently in the mind of the reps who may be hundreds of miles away and selling a variety of other items.

Most companies have sales managers. Those with large numbers of independent sales representatives should also have a manager devoted only to sourcing, training, and making sales calls with the reps. Any rep organization must be managed to be effective. Otherwise, they just take an order, collect a commission from your company, and have little incentive to actively promote your products and services.

Independent sales representatives can give your company a sales force and geographic coverage you could not usually duplicate with full-time employees. The commissions you pay those reps, however, are only a portion of the related expenses. Make those expenses count, and remember that whether a sales rep firm or individual is effective is as much up to you as to them.

146

Chapter 54 - Noncompete and Employment Agreements

Early in my corporate finance career, I was engaged to sell a relatively small company in Orlando. After finding a particularly appropriate candidate for my client's company, we exchanged Confidentiality Agreements, and I then sent the Corporate Profile I had prepared for the company I was selling. Somewhat late in the discussions and after several visits to the seller's company, we suddenly stopped hearing from the potential buyer's president and were not successful in contacting him.

It was only about a month later when the potential buyer hired the principal second-tier executive from the seller's company. The buyer had what he wanted, and the value of the seller's business dropped. From that experience, I learned two valuable lessons. First, my form of Confidentiality Agreement for business transactions has, since that time, contained a strong non-solicitation clause. The confidentiality portion protects the information exchanged during the transaction process. The non-solicitation provision says that neither the buyer nor the seller will hire employees of the other during a period of three years from the date of the agreement.

The second lesson was the value of noncompetition agreements with employees, even for relatively small, non-technical companies. You've spent much time, effort, and money training the various members of your company's staff. During that time, they have also learned much about your company, its operations, and its markets. When one of those employees leaves, should they be completely free to compete with your company and to use against you all of that training and information you gave them? I don't think so.

Although noncompete and non-solicitation agreements are too rarely used, at some companies they are a requirement of being hired and are signed by all employees. Those agreements must, however, be drafted with some care by an attorney with experience in such matters.

In general, a noncompete agreement with an employee cannot provide unreasonable limits on his or her ability to make a living working for some other company. If ever presented to a court for enforcement, the primary criteria will be whether the limits on competition are, or are not, reasonable.

In that regard, the agreement cannot be too broad or be effective over too extensive an area. For instance, if your company's business, including your sales, is conducted principally in Texas, a noncompete agreement that encompasses the entire United States would probably be judged as inappropriate. It could, however, include all of Texas.

147

In defining competition, the agreement must not preclude the employee from working for companies which produce or sell items or services related, but not directly competitive, to those offered by your company. The agreement should be as narrowly focused as feasible but specific as to the types of jobs, the types of companies, and in what geographic areas the employee must not work. Obviously, it should also make your employees cognizant of the value your company places on its proprietary information, operating methods, and markets.

Of course, these agreements with your company's employees should also contain non-solicitation clauses. These clauses should apply not only to hiring or soliciting your other employees but should also apply to soliciting your customers. A former employee should be prevented from hiring the people you've found and trained at significant expense and from calling on the customers you've attracted over the years.

In addition, any noncompete agreement with employees must not be so onerous as to make your own hiring process unduly difficult. As with many aspects of business, drafting an appropriate noncompete agreement for your employees is a balancing act between providing adequate protection for your company and having a contract that is narrow enough to be enforced by the courts but not one that will keep you from hiring talented people either in or outside of your industry.

Any consideration of employee noncompete agreements also leads into the question of employment agreements in general. When I am buying companies for my clients, I always include employment agreements for the sellers, if they are to remain employees after the closing, and for other key employees, if they are important to the future success of the company being acquired. Those agreements, usually providing for terms of three to five years, give the key employees some comfort that the acquisition will not result in their dismissal. They also outline the employee's position and area of direct responsibility and often include specific performance targets which are used to define termination for non-performance.

Over the years, the primary problems I've found with the majority of employment agreements is their negative slant. Those agreements should not dwell only on the items which will cause the employee to be dismissed or to be in violation of the agreement. They should also include incentives such as specifying annual salary reviews, outlining or defining any bonus plan for the employee, and if appropriate, a stock option plan in which the employee may participate.

The employment agreement should also define the employee benefits the company provides including any benefits specific to the position covered such as an automobile or a related allowance. It should also include a provision for extending the agreement after its initial term. After all, when an employment

148

agreement expires, you don't want the employee to leave. You want to either extend the original agreement or draft a new one that recognizes changes in either the company or the key employee's position and responsibilities.

In addition, of course, employment agreements should also include appropriate noncompetition, non-solicitation, and confidentiality provisions unless those are covered in a separate agreement. Properly drafted, employment agreements can not only offer your company significant protection but can also serve as both protection and incentive for your key employees.

149

Chapter 55 - Job Descriptions

C ommon sense would tell us that those who work with and for us should understand their jobs and their specific areas of responsibility. But do they? For years, I have advocated that all companies install a system of developing and periodically updating written job descriptions for all management and supervisory positions. Properly organized, these will not only outline the various jobs within your company but will also give each member of your management team an opportunity to discuss their job and how both of you view that job.

To do this, you can't simply draft job descriptions for each of the key people in your company or department. That would only tell you what you expect in regard to that job or the person who holds it. It would tell you nothing about whether your views are either correct or are shared by the job holder. A much better method of developing job descriptions is to produce a form that outlines the basic information any job description should cover. That information should include:

- The job title
- The person to whom that job holder reports
- The supervisory positions and other employees who report to the job holder
- A description of the job and its areas of responsibility in no more than 250 words
- A description of the authority the job holder can exercise in no more than 100 words
- The name of the current job holder (and author of the job description) and the date

You can then give that form to each of the people who report to you and ask that they describe their own job. After those are complete, you can meet with each employee to review and discuss the job description they've developed. That discussion will give you an opportunity to not only learn how those reporting to you think about their areas of responsibility and authority but will also give you a comparison of how you and the employee feel about their own job.

Those discussions should result in an understanding with each management level employee as to their job description, areas of responsibility, and extent of corporate authority. In addition, the original job description prepared by the

150

employee should then be modified by the employee to coincide with any changes that were decided during the review meeting.

By the way, those job descriptions should match the organization chart for your company which we discussed in Chapter 29.

The job descriptions you develop with your managers and supervisors should also be a part of their personal files and should be reviewed with each manager and updated on an annual basis. That update can be a part of the annual performance review you should also have with each employee reporting to you.

When a management level employee leaves or retires, the job description you've developed and refined with him or her over the years can then help in hiring a replacement. The job description can become the basis for a help wanted internet posting and, in its more complete form, can be given to prospective employees and then discussed with them during job interviews.

Preparing written job descriptions is neither a time consuming nor onerous task. As they are developed, discussed, and refined, however, you may be surprised at the differences between what you think of a person's job and how that person defines it. In that regard, written job descriptions can give every member of your company's management team an excellent opportunity to agree as to the job they are expected to do as well as the responsibilities and authority associated with that job. In addition, the job descriptions can then be used as a part of defining the job performance both expected and delivered.

151

Chapter 56 - Outside Advisors

There are three members of your company's executive team who are not employees but who are almost as important to its development and future as any other executive. They are your corporate attorney, outside accountant, and insurance agent. As defacto members of your management team, they should be kept well advised of your corporate activities, plans, problems, and changes.

In that regard, it's a good practice to meet with each of those key advisors on a periodic but regularly scheduled basis. Depending upon your company's development and resulting corporate growth, these meetings should generally be held with your attorney and accountant once each quarter and with your insurance agent twice a year. Between meetings, these advisors should each receive your monthly financial statements with a note explaining any significant developments or changes to either line items or your company's overall financial results.

Those three advisors should also be either appointed as directors or invited to attend all directors' meetings as observers. Whether they can serve as directors or simply attend the meetings will depend upon their required autonomy in the case of accountants or their firm's policies regarding such corporate relationships.

Your attorney should not only be consulted but should also participate in any significant corporate development. Of course, those would include a review function for all contracts other than routine customer matters; any consideration of an acquisition, merger, or significant corporate relationship; and both short-term and long-term planning for growth or reactions to market changes.

In addition, it's a good idea to review with your corporate attorney, on at least an annual basis, your company's By-Laws and its Articles of Incorporation or corporate organization and structure. (Also see Chapter 24.) Although changes to those corporate documents may not be needed every year, when a change is indicated, it should be made on a timely basis.

Over the years, I've frequently been involved in acquisitions, company sales, or capital raising efforts for which the corporate organization and related documentation was either insufficient or simply wrong. The result was a rush to make necessary changes, some of which, on occasion, delayed a critical closing. I've also had client companies that used their attorneys to cure legal problems which wouldn't have occurred had changes been made earlier.

152

The solution is easy; treat your corporate attorney as a member of your executive team. The advice and attention you receive will be well worth any minor fees associated with the time your attorney spends maintaining current contact with the members of your management group and an up-to-date knowledge of your plans, developments, and problems.

In regard to periodic contacts with your outside accountant, those should center around discussions of any financial reporting matters, tax questions, changes in general accounting principals which might effect your company and, of course, an analysis of its financial ratios, strength, and need for additional growth capital. Just as you review corporate organizational matters with your attorney, you should also involve your outside accountant in reviewing your company's financial results, internal accounting controls, and any past or planned changes that might effect those financial results.

As mentioned in Chapter 45, when accountants perform annual audits for their clients, they often include in those services a "management letter". This is simply a report to management which is outside the normal audit process. The report covers any financial or other deficiencies the auditors might have found during their investigation of the company's annual financial statements and related results. I have long felt that this management letter can be more important than the audit report. As a result, you should ask your outside accountant to prepare such a letter each year, even if he or she is only "reviewing" your annual statements rather than conducting a full audit.

When considering the outside advisors to your company who should be treated as members of your executive team, few managers think of their insurance agent. That agent, however, is an integral part of your company's risk management functions and is important to considering how your corporate risks should be either minimized or covered by insurance. (Also see Chapter 47.)

In addition to considering coverage which your company may lack, it may also have coverage that is either redundant or not cost effective. Your insurance agent is the best person to give you advice as to your company's insurance, the premium cost related to the covered risks, and any changes in your coverage which should be made as your company grows.

Another insurance matter that can be of particular importance is life insurance for key executives, often called "key man insurance" prior to the emphasis on politically correct gender titles. Ask yourself what would be the financial effect of a loss of any of your company's key management personnel, including yourself. Because term life insurance is usually inexpensive, such key man policies can be a cost effective method of covering such a loss, hiring a replacement, or providing the funds needed for a stock repurchase obligation.

153

Your company's managers and its employees are among its most valuable assets. That team of people who are the foundation for your company's future should also include your outside advisors. Use those advisors wisely and consult with them often.

154

Chapter 57 - Personal Organization

I was in a lady's office not long ago and saw a plaque on her desk that read, "A Clean Desk is a Sign of a Sick Mind". I'm surprised that I saw it; the clutter almost engulfed the entire room. When I mentioned that plaque to my wife, she replied that I must, in that case, have a particularly sick mind. I'm excessively organized, but I find that it helps. Time that would otherwise be lost can be applied to productive tasks, and prioritized lists allow me to get the most important work done first.

A good motto is "Keep it Organized; Keep it Clean; Keep it Neat; Keep it Orderly". Doing that will not only make your life easier but will also give you that rarest of commodities: more time to devote to both business and pleasure. Of course, business can also be a pleasure which makes it easier as well as more productive.

Some years ago, I had a client whose company produced several specialty food products. I was always stunned by his personal office space. He was not only a smoker who never seemed to empty an ashtray but also allowed paper to accumulate over months, if not years. I found it difficult to believe that he could adequately manage any company and, in particular, a food production facility.

Although there may be no direct link between the disorderly state of his office and his company's performance, that operation did start to contract and is today a significantly smaller company. That failure, I believed, had something to do with the owner's inability to organize his own affairs and to keep his personal space clean and orderly.

Because I've had a number of clients over the years in various metal machining and fabrication businesses, I've conducted a most unscientific survey related to their level of profits. I've generally found that those facilities with swept floors and no accumulated scrap had higher profits than their messier competitors. The shops that looked like neglected junk yards produced lower profits, if any at all.

In today's world of PDAs (Personal Digital Assistants), electronic calendars, multiple computer generated lists, favorites, and e-mail contact addresses, staying organized should be easy. Many people, however, still don't or can't do it. That presents the question as to whether organization can be learned or is only inherited; is it nature or nurture; genetic, taught, or habit? I like to think that personal organization can, at least to some substantial extent, be learned.

Years ago, I developed a Microsoft Word based call list form. Ever since, I've updated that list at the end of every day to show all current contacts and the calls I should make the following day. I also developed a Microsoft Excel based calendar that shows the current and next seven weeks on a single page. At the end of each day, I color the background for the day just ended using the Excel "fill" option. At the end of each week, I delete the top rows for that week and add rows at the bottom for the eighth week on the page. Although there are numerous computer calendars, I like the one I designed for the way I work.

Both my call list and my calendar are always on my computer, cell phone, and desk. I have long found that, if you're well organized, you can join what I consider an elite group of generally productive people. If you're not organized, you can use your own experience to determine if that talent can or cannot be learned. Learning it will be helpful to you and increase your personal productivity.

Henry Mintzberg, a twentieth century business professor, said that "Management is, above all, a practice where art, science, and craft meet." I would add to that "...and are then organized to produce a desired result rather than allowed to conflict one with the other." Think about your personal organization and how you might add productive time to your day without adding any more work or hours. It's not hard to do, and it sure makes your work easier, shorter, and less tedious.

156

Chapter 58 - Outsourcing

O ver the past few years, I've heard much controversy about outsourcing. Most of that discussion has centered around the cost advantage of buying products or services overseas contrasted with the negative and politically charged question of sending American jobs to foreign countries. Both of those aspects of outsourcing, however, are only a part of the consideration and, on occasion, are not even the most important part

Certainly, the pet food companies during early 2007 found that their cost advantage from buying products in China over a number of years was more than eliminated by the cost of the resulting product recall when pets started dying from tainted food. In regard to sending American jobs overseas, however, some companies must do that in order to preserve the jobs of their employees who are involved in every aspect of their business other than manufacturing.

Several years ago, I had a client whose company manufactured scuba diving equipment. Because it was one of the smaller producers in that market, it was forced to follow the pricing policies of its much later competitors. Without purchasing some of its products and principal components from overseas suppliers, my client's company could not have remained competitive. Over the last few years, it began to increase the foreign content of its products.

It also found, however, that the U.S. military wanted a domestic manufacturer to supply much of its underwater equipment. Today, that company is larger and provides more American based jobs than in its entire history. Its manufacturing operations are smaller, but its fulfillment, sales, testing, and inventory operations are significantly larger. Without outsourcing appropriate components and products and sending those manufacturing jobs overseas, that company wouldn't exist today. Instead, its employment rolls have continued to grow in all aspects of the business except, of course, for that portion of its manufacturing done in China.

When considering outsourcing for any aspect of your products, don't just look at the relative cost of domestic versus foreign production. Consider carefully each aspect of the outsourcing decision. Among those, include:

Quality - My scuba equipment client found that certain of its products were of higher quality from its overseas supplier than from its own production. This was particularly true for the buoyancy compensators which were sewn much like clothing. It also found, however, that some complex assemblies, such as air tank regulators, were better assembled and tested in its own facility using overseas components. That company developed a domestic/overseas production mix that allowed it to maintain its reputation for the highest quality scuba gear while taking advantage of lower overseas production costs.

157

Cost - When comparing the cost of domestic and overseas production, be sure to include all of the related costs for both sources. Of course, in addition to the product cost, these include product shipping expenses, the added inventory carrying costs required for larger overseas orders, letters of credit for payments to the foreign suppliers, any additional fulfillment expenses associated with warehousing and repacking, periodic travel to your suppliers facilities, any added insurance costs, and, of course, the business risks associated with using a supplier on the other side of the world.

Risks - In regard to the business risks of using any third-party supplier, the risks associated with overseas manufacturers can include placing the reputation of your company and its product quality in the hands of a foreign company you don't and can't control.

My scuba gear client was careful to make sure that it controlled, in its own facility and with its own people, the testing and quality of those equipment items that relate to personal safety several hundred feet under water. It took advantage of lower overseas costs but maintained control over the risks associated with using its foreign suppliers.

Customer Service - When I last purchased a relatively high end computer for my office use, I called both Dell and HP to discuss the specifications and features I needed. I bought an HP Compaq. That turned out to be an easy decision. The Dell representative spoke poor English at best; the HP representative was talking with me from a call center in Pennsylvania. That made a big difference.

I recently had a client in the telephone answering business. That service market has undergone substantial changes over the years as voice mail, e-mail, answering machines, and text messaging have encroached on remote answering. As that market contracted, the remaining users were those people who needed a telephone response that was controlled by a person actually talking with the caller. Of course, those include doctors who need the person answering the phone to exercise some judgment as to how the call should be handled.

My telephone answering service client has now set up a system of call transfers to a Philippine service center and intends to sell that lower cost service to other telephone answering companies. I wonder, however, if a physician and others who have chosen a person over a machine to handle their calls will want to have their phone answered by someone with less than a complete command of the English language. The results of that outsourcing effort aren't yet apparent, but I anticipate that the minor cost advantage of a foreign call center will not compensate for the lower customer service that might result.

Inventory - Most overseas suppliers require container size orders. Those large shipments can not only result in high inventory carrying costs but also increase the risk that a delayed shipment might cause you to lose orders or damage your customer relationship.

Competition - Don't neglect to consider and use product or service outsourcing where such foreign supply either offers your company a competitive advantage or allows it to compete with others already using less expensive overseas sources. If your company doesn't remain competitive, you put the jobs of all your employees at risk.

Any manufacturing company should continually assess its "make or buy" options related not only to overseas suppliers but also to domestic companies that might produce a component or a complete product less expensively or with higher quality that it can in its own facilities. These "make or buy" decisions can determine whether your company grows or stagnates and disappears. (Also see Chapters 9 and 52.)

Outsourcing, however, isn't only a matter of cost. It relates to every aspect of the supply of your company's products or services, your relationships with your customers, and the risks associated with your markets and operations. Outsourcing isn't a matter of whether or not to ship American jobs overseas but how to best manage your business and supply your customers with quality products and services at competitive prices. Do that and your company will prosper. You'll add jobs, even if they aren't in your manufacturing or service operations.

159

Chapter 59 - Policies & Procedures

We've talked previously about various aspects of insurance and risk management. (See Chapter 47.) There is, however, a form of business insurance that does not come as a policy with specific coverage. It is not only good insurance against future litigation but is also an integral part of good management. That is a company Policy Handbook. In today's litigious world, it's not enough to be against sexual harassment, racial preferences, and other unacceptable employee or corporate behavior. Every company needs to have written policies defining its opposition to such behavior and setting out its corporate policies and restrictions related to such conduct.

Twenty or thirty years ago, it was almost standard to find pinups, itself an archaic word, spread among the machinery on any shop floor. The Rigid Tool Company was even known for its annual pinup calendar that almost every machine shop and construction job site displayed in various locations. Today, that is clearly unacceptable.

If your company doesn't have a written Policy Handbook which is given to all employees, it should. In addition to establishing your company's positions regarding what is and is not acceptable employee behavior, that Handbook can also be used to describe employee benefits, vacation and holiday practices, paid and unpaid time off, promotion policies, how seniority is handled and its various benefits, and reasons for dismissal other than poor performance.

Once that Handbook is written and distributed, it should then become the corporate standard with a demonstrated adherence to its policies. In the event of an employee law suit against the company for any employment related matter, that Handbook will become a valuable defense, but only if it has actually been used and not just written and distributed.

Another corporate handbook that every company should have is a collection of written procedures and guidelines. You expect your company's employees to each know their job, but there's always some turnover of personnel. An incoming person may not approach a job in the same way as the previous person. In either case, your company should have established procedures describing how its principal jobs should be handled.

The best method of compiling such a Procedure Manual is to ask each person responsible for a specific task to write a short paragraph or section of the Manual describing their job, how it should be handled, and, its relationship to other jobs or procedures. (Also see Chapter 55.) Each manager can then review the procedures for his or her department, revise them, and submit them for incorporation in the complete Corporate Procedure Manual.

Among other topics, the Manual should cover:

- Requisitions, purchasing, the approvpal process, receiving, and vendor invoice approvals
- Inventory controls, inventory withdrawal requests, perpetual inventory methods, and periodic physical counts
- Accounting, revenue recognition, accruals, depreciation policies, expense allocations (usually none), and other accounting procedures
- Budgets and budgeting procedures
- Distribution of monthly financial statements and other financial control information
- Annual accounting audit or review procedures
- Collection procedures and methods, invoice terms, and bad debt recognition
- Banking, finance, bonding, credit line borrowing base calculations, check signing and signers, and the loan approval process
- Insurance, coverage limits, deductibles, and related policy terms
- Safety policies and procedures, risk management, and safety training
- Employee training and apprenticeship programs
- Human resources, employee files, noncompetition agreements, employment agreements, and hiring and termination procedures
- A corporate organization chart and procedures for the preparation and review of written job descriptions
- Sales management, product or service pricing and approval procedures, and project pricing or bid preparation, approval, and submittals
- Client contract provisions, standard sales order terms and conditions, and both payment and discount provisions
- Customer, vendor, and other outside communications
- All aspects of internal employee communications, deficiency and problem notices or notification, dispute resolution, and employee suggestions
- Quality controls and product or service level inspections and reporting
- Warranty requests, approvals, and related warranty work
- Outsourcing policies and procedures
- Confidentiality, intellectual property protection, and noncompetition policies
- Updating both the Corporate Policy Handbook and the Procedure Manual
- And any other policies or procedures which are important to your specific business or operations

161

Both the Corporate Policy Handbook and the Procedure Manual should be reviewed no less than annually and then revised, updated, reprinted, and distributed to all management personnel. As your company grows and adds additional people, departments, and operations, its management will become both more complex and more widely disbursed. It will be increasingly important to assure that corporate policies and procedures are uniform, well understood, and followed at all levels within your company.

Simple, concise, and published corporate policies and procedures will be invaluable in building a smoothly functioning organization in which the individuals know their jobs and approach them in a uniform and effective manner.

162

Chapter 60 - From My Wife

Some who have read this book have asked about me, my past work, and how I think about management. So for that topic, it's my wife's turn.

Things I've learned about Lee's this book won't tell you

Having been married to Lee Rust for well over 20 years now, during all of which he has been a self-employed business consultant working from home, I've learned a few interesting things about business and my husband. Here are some of my observations about Lee's world:

According to Lee, the number one rule of business is "No one will ever return your call, so keep calling them until they do." And he's relentless. If he says he will call on a certain day, he will call. If he has to leave a message, he'll wait a "Lee Rust amount of time", maybe an hour, and then call again. My advice; call him back. He'll never go away.

- You've probably heard of island time. Around here we run on "Lee Rust Time." That is, an arrival to an appointment on time is the same as being late. If he says 1:00 o'clock, he'll be there at 12:45, if not sooner.

- If it wasn't in The Wall Street Journal, it didn't happen.

- There are only two kinds of lawyers; deal doers and deal killers. Lee's not fond of the second.

- Angel investors in the business world are as hard to find as the winged variety.

- After all the analysis, graphs, and charts have been produced, evaluated, and discussed, the true value of a company is exactly what someone is willing to pay for it.

- I've learned that 5 times EBITDA is not a new rock band, an Asian appetizer, or a horse running in the 5th, but rather an accounting formula for calculating a company's purchase price.

- The business world is full of euphemisms. "Economies of scale" translates to "somebody is gonna get laid off". "There are many ways we can structure a deal" means "This is not going to be a cash heavy transaction." And "conservative estimates of profits" means "this is what our company will make next year if Venus aligns with Mars."

- It is possible to graduate from Yale and have an incurable inability to spell. Lee views spellchecker as one of man's greatest inventions.

- If you call Lee at 6:00 a.m., he's at his desk. If you call him at 5:00 p.m., he's probably cooking dinner. If you call him at 9:00 pm, his wife gets really irate.

- If he starts a sentence with "my father always told me", be prepared for a joke that's not going to be very funny.

If you tell Lee a joke or use an expression that is connected to something on television, he will look at you with an absolutely blank stare. He knows TV was invented, but doesn't understand why.

Working from home requires acute powers of concentration, especially when the grandchildren are visiting. Fortunately, Lee is able to tune out noisy distractions, even preschooler computer games, although I do live in fear that someday a client will receive a document that contains a clause that says "Click the blue triangle that has 9 yellow dots" or "Can you help Boo Boo Chicken find his way home?"

Finally, I've learned that most troubled companies have weak accounting departments. All successful companies have well-run, accurate, accounting departments that pay their business consultant's invoices swiftly.

My wife is a great manager; she manages our house and me with me being the harder part

Chapter 61 - Real Estate Ownership

I have on occasion advised some of my clients to separate their land and buildings from their operating company and then lease those facilities back to the company. Although not appropriate in all circumstances, there is a strong rationale for that separation. If you have any intention of selling your company within the foreseeable future, the price you receive may be substantially higher if the business does not own the physical facilities it uses but leases those facilities from you or from a trust or related investor group that you might form.

In many, if not most, cases the purchase price for a business is based on a multiple of its earnings or of its EBITDA (Earnings Before Interest, Taxes, Depreciation, and Amortization). When using those calculations of value, however, the price to be paid for the business is usually changed to only a minor extent by whether the business does or does not own its buildings. Although the calculations and comparison can be complex, the effect of the lease expense on the earnings, and therefore the value, is often offset by the combination of interest expense on the mortgage and the assumption of the mortgage by the buyer. As a result, the business is valued based only on its earnings or EBITDA, and the seller does not receive the full value for the real property.

However, if the real property and the business operations are separate, the business can be sold with the price based on its earnings. The seller can then either continue to lease the building to the buyer as an additional income source or sell the building to the buyer in a separate but related transaction. In that instance, the building would be sold with the price based on its appraised value at the time of the sale.

The sum of the value or sales price for the business plus the appraised value or sale price for the land and buildings is almost always greater than the sales price for the business and buildings combined. Of course, in Florida, my home state, the sales tax on leases is a deterrent to separating the real property from the business. Even with that penalty, however, if the business might be sold within a determinate number of years, the increased return from selling the businesses and its facility in separate but related transactions will usually more than compensate for the sales taxes that have been paid.

If your company is taxed as a Sub-Chapter S Corporation or is structured as an LLC, the separation of the real property from the business should not introduce significant tax problems. That is, however, not the case for a "C" corporation. That notwithstanding, even for a C corporation, the separation of the real property from the operating business should be explored.

165

Chapter 62 - An Operations Audit

Because the future is always cloudy; this might be a particularly good time to review your operations and do some planning for that future.

Every year, you have your outside accountants review or audit your financial statements, but have you ever thought of auditing your operations? After all, the efficiency of those operations largely determines your company's financial results. In addition to simply exploring the efficiencies, or lack of efficiencies, in your operations, an Operations Audit can also be used to explore:

- How each element or business segment of your organization functions and how they should function over the next three to five years;
- Your company's corporate and operational strengths and weaknesses and how to cure the weaknesses;
- Identifying both your company's efficiencies and its inefficiencies, and how to address the inefficiencies;
- How your employees communicate and work together (or are at odds with one another);
- The application of daily, weekly, and monthly internal controls to monitor and improve your operations;
- How to increase sales and, therefore, both revenues and profits;
- What other growth opportunities exist and how to explore and use those that are appropriate;
- And other options for improvements in your operations, organization, and financial results.

In regard to your company's operating efficiencies, you might find it instructive to calculate the LER (Labor Efficiency Ratio) for your company as a whole and for any of its various segments that can be separated. The LER is simply your direct labor costs divided by the total revenues that labor produced. By calculating that ratio each month, you can not only measure your labor efficiency trend over time but can also judge the effect on that ratio of changes you might make in our organization or operating methods.

Don't do things tomorrow the way you do them today unless you're absolutely sure they're the best way. You examine your company's financial results each month. Now start examining its individual operations and measure what each of those operations contributes to both their individual segment of the business and its overall results.

166

Chapter 63 - Incentive Compensation

I have long been a proponent of incentive compensation. Rewards work. In addition, an incentive compensation plan that gives key employees higher pay also acts as a golden handcuff. They might get a similar or higher salary working for one of your competitors but could they also match their incentive payments?

Setting up an incentive compensation plan is not difficult nor complex. In fact, any such plan should be simple, easy to understand, and based on no more than one or two criteria. Choosing those criteria, however, are one of the most important aspects of the plan. They should be easily measured performance indicators that can clearly be controlled by the employee and that will result in higher profits for the company. After all, the incentive should be self-funding; that is the payment to the employee should represent only a reasonable percentage of the return to the company from that employee's superior performance.

In addition, the criteria should be one that is an important determinant of the company's profits as well as one that can and should be improved. Several years ago, I developed an incentive compensation plan for a CPA firm. In discussing those metrics that effected both the company' s revenues and profits, I determined that one of the most important was the percentage of available hours that were actually billed to clients by each of the firm's professional staff. In addition, their billing percentages appeared to be lower than those of other firms and also showed too much variation between individuals.

The objective of the incentive compensation plan was not only to increase the hours billed but also to reward those professionals who had the highest billable percentages. By building a simple, economic model of the incentive plan, I was able to show the effect for the individual employees and for the company from specific changes in the percentage of billable hours for each producer. Based on those models, I then worked with the firm's managing partner to set the level of reward for each percentage point improvement. In addition, we were able to establish specific incentive compensation targets for each type of income producing employee.

For another of my clients, a multi-branch distributor, in addition to the individual branch contribution to overhead and profits, another important criteria turned out to be the level of inventory held by each branch as a percent of its revenues. By lowering that percentage, the company could generate higher cash flow, lower the use of their bank credit line, and therefore, generate higher profits. The two criteria that were then used to establish each branch manager's incentive compensation were branch profits as well as the

167

---

percentage of the branch's inventory to its sales within specific "out of stock" revenue loss ratios.

For salespeople who are often compensated with commissions, how those incentive commissions are calculated are particularly important. If the salesperson has any control over the product pricing, incentives related to the revenues generated by the salesperson can be counterproductive. There would be an incentive to lower prices in order to increase sales and, therefore, the salesperson's incentive compensation level. That, however, is not in the company's best interest.

In those cases, it is better to base the incentive compensation on the gross profits generated by each salesperson and not on the sales levels. In that way, those individuals who produce the highest profits will be rewarded.

For any incentive compensation plan, determine those measures of success that can and should be improved recognizing that they may be different for different types of employees. Then for each class of employee model the economic effect for both the individual and the company. That model can then be used to test various levels of incentive payments and to choose those that are most beneficial to the company but still act as a significant incentive for the employee.

Again, rewards work; they can and should be used to help most companies reach their growth and profit objectives.

168

Chapter 64 - Banking Relationships (continued)

"**B**anks aren't lending." How often have I heard that and thought, "That's not true"? It is true, however, that banks are no longer offering the easy credit of the earlier and mid 2000's, 125% loan to equity and low doc mortgages, no verification loans, and other silly lending policies that contributed to the worst recession since 1929.

Although it was painfully slow, that recession has ended, and banks are lending again but hopefully with more stringent requirements related to their borrower's repayment ability. After all, the profits generated by banks accrue principally from lending money to credit worthy customers, both commercial and personal.

In regard to your ability to get (or maintain) bank financing for working capital, expansion plans, acquisitions, or other projects that require more funds than your company has on hand, much depends on your banking relationship. As mentioned in Chapter 42, you need to work to keep that relationship in good order. That is important enough to repeat.

Bankers hate surprises and love financial and operating information. Treat your banker accordingly. Put your principal bank representative on your regular mailing list for your company's monthly financial statements. If you have a problem, don't just send the financials, or even worse not send them at all; hand carry a copy to your banker and explain what caused the problem and what you have done or will do to correct it.

In your financial package, it is also a good idea to include projections for future performance and a comparison of your company's current results with those projections. By the way, don't use annual projections. Those assume that nothing changes throughout the year. Make your revenue and expense forecasts by quarter for one or two years in the future. Then track your performance against that budget each month and update your forecasts each quarter. (Also see Chapters 19 and 20.)

As to acquisition or project financing, compile a comprehensive business plan for the project. That plan, of course, should include the historical financials for an acquisition plus projections of the anticipated new operations as a part of your company. Projections should also be used for any other type of expansion project. In all cases, the plan should include a detailed Source & Use of Funds table. Send the plan to your banker and schedule a meeting to discuss it in detail. That should be a sales meeting; you are selling your banker on the validity of your plans and the future of your company.

The care and feeding of your banker is an integral part of your company's growth and development. Treat him or her accordingly.

169

Is This Any Way to Run a Company?   H. Lee Rust

Chapter 65 - Shell Company Mergers

For years I've followed with interest the concept of "shell company deals". Those transactions offer a method for a private company to become publicly owned, not through an IPO (Initial Public Offering) but by merging with a public shell company.

Such a shell company is one that is publicly owned and has a sufficient number of stockholders to require SEC reporting. For various reasons, however, the shell company has no operations, no business, and in most cases, no assets other than its public ownership and SEC reporting status. By merging with such a public shell, a private company gains public ownership without the high cost of an IPO. The original owners of the public shell company then become minor minority owners in the merger partner, and the combined company is then, of course, an operating public owned company.

In general, there are two primary reasons, among others, for a private company to become publicly owned. First, it can be an attractive method of raising capital funds without incurring additional debt. And second, the public ownership and related share trading market can provide liquidity for the company's owners.

That is the theory, but for a shell company merger, the reality is quite different. By merging with a public shell company which has no assets, the private company gains no additional funding and, in fact, incurs certain, if not all, of the expenses associated with public ownership.

In addition, being publicly owned does not mean that the stockholders gain any liquidity for their ownership interest. For that liquidity, a market for the shares must be developed and maintained. That's relatively easy if the company qualifies for an exchange listing such as Nasdaq, but if it doesn't, the stock may be listed on the "Bulletin Board' or, worse yet, the "Pink Sheets". Neither of those listings offers any real liquidity.

In fact, any publicly owned company which does not have the minimum requirements for a Nasdaq Capital Market listing (generally for smaller companies) should not be publicly owned. A company with its shares listed on either the Bulletin Board or the Pink Sheets will have all of the disadvantages and costs of being publicly owned but without any of the principal advantages of that public status. If the private company has the minimum requirements for Nasdaq and needs the contributions public ownership can offer, it should do an IPO, not merge with a shell company.

In regard to capital formation and growth opportunities for small and medium sized companies, a shell company merger is never, in my experience, an attractive alternative. Happily there are many other options that can be used. (Also see Chapter 14.)

Chapter 66 - Accounting versus Internal Controls

As I mentioned in Chapter 5, a recurring problem in many small and medium sized companies is inadequate internal financial controls. The reason for that deficiency is also easy: Companies are most often started by entrepreneurs and entrepreneurs are seldom accountants. If your monthly financial statements have been designed for accounting purposes, work with your comptroller or accountant to redesign them for use by you and your management team. For that redesign, several suggestions include:

- If your monthly statements are more than fifteen days old, they aren't control tools but are merely historical curiosities. Change that.
- Use profit center accounting for any portion of the business that can be separated as to revenues, costs, and either gross or net profits. Then those profit centers should be independently monitored and controlled. Usually, however, only one consolidated balance sheet is needed for the entire company.
- Try to present each profit center income statement (or the entire company's income statement) on no more than one or two pages. If that can't be done, try to identify individual line items that can or should be combined.
- Identify those expense items most subject to your control, and then concentrate on understanding those and their trends.
- All line items should have a column for percent of revenues. That allows you to track trends when dollar amounts change.
- Do you really care about the amount of payroll taxes? No, what's important is the total compensation costs, including those taxes and all employee benefits.
- If you manage a company with $5 million of annual revenues, is any line item of less than $5,000 important? No, condense them.
- Don't list the expense items alphabetically; list them by importance to your profits, usually the highest to lowest dollar amounts.

Concentrate your financial reporting on items you can control and can understand the effects of those controls on profits. The principal management use for your company's monthly financial statements should be controls over revenues and expenses that you can use to measure and enhance results.

By the way, why wait until month end? On the next page I will include a Weekly Financial Report that highlights important trends and shows a concentration on cash control. This report should be compiled by your accounting department each Monday morning for the close of business the previous Friday. It should then be distributed to each member of the management staff.

171

XYZ Manufacturing Company

Weekly Financial Report - As of Friday, _____, 2016

	Beginning Balance Monday	Deposits Made	Payments Made	Current Balance Friday	
Bank Cash Position					

	Beginning Loan Balance	Draws Taken	Payments Made	Current Loan Balance	
Bank Credit Line **Today**					

Estimated Total Qualifying Assets:		
Estimated Loan Funds Available:		

Accounts Receivable	1 - 30 Days	30 - 60 Days	60 - 90 Days	Over 90 Days	Totals
January 1, 2016					
1st of this Month					
Today					

Projected Payments	Payroll	Taxes	Payables	Other	Total
Next Week					

Accounts Payable	1 - 30 Days	30 - 60 Days	Total		
January 1, 2016				**Projected Receipts This Week**	
1st of this Month				**Projected Payments**	
Today				**Difference**	

Sales Data	Dollars	**Current Backlog**	Dollars	**Margin**	Percent
Sales Last Week		Orders Rec'd Last Week		Budget	
Month to Date		Other Unfilled Orders		Actual	
Year to Date		Total Backlog			

Head Count	Administration	Production	Sales	Engineering	Totals
January 1, 2016					
1st of this Month					
Today					

Pending Cash Needs: Amount

Payment Date: _____ Item: _____ $ _____

Comments: _____

Payment Date: _____ Item: _____ $ _____

Comments: _____

Other Comments: _____

_____

172

Chapter 67 - Building Depreciation

If either you or your company (or for attorneys and accountants, any of your clients) own the building you use for its operations, here is a modest tax savings that might be worth exploring. Rather than depreciate the building at its purchase or construction price over 15 to 30 years, divide it into its individual parts. That is, separate the climate control system, water heaters, compressed air equipment and piping, water and waste water system, electrical distribution equipment, and any other mechanical components from the building structure.

Then with a professional opinion as to the value of each component, you may be able to establish a shorter life on much, if not all, of the mechanical and other systems.   The air conditioning system, for instance, should depreciate over a much shorter time than the building structure. To the extent that you can accelerate the depreciation period for any of those components, your depreciation charges (a non-cash expense) will go up, and your taxes will go down.

It is worth considering. Start by talking with your accountant or corporate attorney. Then work with them to determine what elements of your physical facilities can be segregated and depreciated at a faster rate than the building.

By the way, I have long contended that operating companies should not own the facilities they use. (See Chapter 61.) If a sale of your company might happen in the foreseeable future, your net proceeds from that sale will be much higher if the building is separated from the operations. With that separation, the company's sales price will be based on its historical earnings and future potential. The building, sold in a separate transaction, will be priced based on its appraised value. In almost all cases, the two separate sales values will dramatically exceed a single price for the operations including the physical facilities.

It is not difficult to compile an economic analysis of that operations/real property separation concept and then compare the resulting enterprise values. Then work with your accountants or attorneys to determine how the land and buildings can be moved into a separate corporate entity also owned by the company owners.

Chapter 68 - Operating Agreements

I have heard from my legal friends that lawyers don't get rich off of 49% / 51% partnerships; lawyers get rich off of 50% / 50% partnerships. That introduces the concept not only of ownership in a closely held corporation but also the need for an Operating Agreement that can be used to control corporate governance. Too often I find that company owners equate their percentage of ownership with control, but that is not always true. An Operating Agreement can be used to determine how a company will be controlled and by whom regardless of the relative ownership percentages of the stockholders.

For that, as well as other reasons, an Operating Agreement is extremely important for any small company, even one that is just starting. When a company is founded and has little value, control issues don't seem particularly important. But wait a few years and success can dramatically increase the importance of clear control policies and procedures.

For many of the Operating Agreements I've drafted, I often include super majority voting provisions. With those, the control over the daily functions of the company are clearly separated from certain important corporate matters. Daily operations are delegated to the various officers of the company. However, corporate decisions, such as a sale of the company, raising addition equity or debt funds, or any change that expands the operations beyond the original core business, require more than a majority vote of either the directors or stockholders. Those super majority vote provisions give minority owners a veto power over the decisions which can have a pronounced effect on the company and its future.

Whether starting a new company or building one that has long been in business, make sure that all of the owners and executives agree as to how the company will be managed, who controls what aspects of that management, and what owners can make the critical corporate decisions. You and your company will be well served by developing a clear and comprehensive Operating Agreement. (Also see chapter 23.)

Chapter 69 - Is Debt Bad?

In the previous chapter, we discussed a company with significant excess working capital. Let's expand on that thought. Several years ago, I had a client in another specialty product manufacturing business. The company had been profitable for years, had no interest bearing debts, and a book value of almost $7 million. The owners were particularly proud of their company's debt free status. However, after reviewing their financial statements, I commented to the principal owner that his lack of debt might not be best for either the company or for him as the owner. He was mystified.

You have a $7 million book value, I explained, and no long term debt. That is over $6 million of unused assets that could be applied to growth, increased profits, and greater enterprise value. Instead, it is wasted, a growth machine not used. Rather than be so proud of a debt free balance sheet, that owner should have looked for growth opportunities, new product lines, an acquisition, or other market expansion possibilities. Then he could borrow against his unused assets to fund that growth.

Too much debt is a problem; too little, however, is also a problem.

I had another client participating in wholesale product sales and distribution. That company had also been profitable for some years, and by using producer consignment inventory, the owners had built a sizable business providing them with relatively high personal compensation. But the company had almost no assets and no book value. Its owners were also proud of their debt free status but that aversion to debt had adversely effected their ability to build value.

Again, the lack of reasonable levels of debt financing had deprived that company of its ability to generate increased enterprise value. In addition, because consignment inventory was more expensive than the cost of debt to finance the purchase of inventory, the company's gross profits were about 15% lower that they would have been with owned inventory.

Is debt bad? Too much debt and the inability to service the debt with profits is certainly bad. But too little debt can also be bad if it results in unused assets or low gross profits. A low debt to equity ratio may be an indication of unused assets. No equity may be an indication of low profits over time and an inability to build assets and value. Debt levels need to be carefully balanced with profit generation, business risks, and growth opportunities, but don't be too proud of a debt free operation. That may only be an indication that you should evaluate new opportunities that reasonable debt levels could help you realize.

175

Chapter 70 - Corporate Character (Continued)

As also outlined in Chapter 49, companies each have a distinct character, just like people do, and over time that corporate character reflects the attitudes and attributes of the senior management team. If a company is managed by several people at the top who are particularly disagreeable, people with a different disposition will not find the atmosphere compatible and will eventually leave. However, those with a personal character matching the top executives will find that they are readily accepted and will blend with the company character that is already in place.

But unlike with some people, a company's character can be changed and can be made to reflect the message you want your company to display to the world. For instance, if customer service is a significant part of your company's operations, make sure that every employee not only understands the importance of customer service but also displays a high level of service even with others who are not customers. The importance of service will permeate all aspects of your operations, and your company will display that character in all of its outside contacts.

Start working on your company's character with a manager's meeting devoted only to a discussion of that character. Ask all members of your management team to come to the meeting with a short written description of (1) how they perceive your company's character and (2) what they believe that character should be. You can then discuss those descriptions as well as those characteristics you believe to be the most important for your company and how they can be adopted and displayed.

By the way, your company's character starts with your receptionist. (Also see Chapter 3.) He or she is often the first contact a customer, potential customer, supplier, or others may have with your company. Make sure that initial contact displays the attitude you want to project to the world. When on hold do you want your customers to hear cop-killer-rap music or a laxative commercial? Is your receptionist curt or accommodating and pleasant; is he or she helpful or disagreeable? And can any caller reaching your company easily talk with a human being and not be caught in an endless chain of computer questions and multiple choice responses?

Make sure the character you want your company to display is understood and projected by every one of its employees. This is important enough to support a little repetition in our book.

176

Chapter 71 - Key Employee Incentive Plans

As I mentioned in Chapter 63, I am a strong advocate of various incentive plans for key managers and employees. In that regard, I thought you would be interested in the following comparison.

Incentive Plan	Advantages	Disadvantages
Discretionary Bonuses	- Payout amount is flexible - No rigid bonus formula - No rigid payout schedule	- Low incentive value - Payout is felt to be arbitrary - Participants can't measure their interim bonus performance
Formula Based Bonus Plans	- Participants can measure their bonus performance - Bonuses can be tailored to individual criteria	- Incentive is for short term performance - Lacks incentive for enterprise value enhancement
ESOP Conversion (Employee Stock Ownership Plan)	- Significant tax savings - Owners set the company value & sales price	- Significant level of government regulation - Inappropriate participants - Low level of incentive value - High future claim on capital - Reduces or eliminates future corporate options
Phantom Stock	- Payout is long term - Low claim on future capital - No corporate governance considerations	- Participants feel they are second class citizens - No method of measuring payout or performance toward payout - Low short term incentive value - Payout occurs only at some indeterminate future time
Conventional Stock Options	- Well understood concept - Payout is long term - Majority of payouts use no company capital - Majority of payouts related only to a liquidity event	- Low, if any, short term incentive value & no short term payout - Participants cannot measure option value or change - Interim conversion requires a method of providing liquidity
Equity Capital Accounts	- Participants can measure performance quarterly - Provides both short and long term incentives - Provides strong "golden handcuffs" for key employees - No corporate governance problems or considerations - Better aligns the managers' and owners' corporate objectives - Well suited for subsidiaries	- Appreciation of value related only to performance by the entire company or subsidiary - Limited short term cash payout for the participants - These accounts are a new, somewhat complex concept

177

Chapter 72 - Equity Capital Accounts

In the chart on the previous page, I mentioned Equity Capital Accounts. Because I developed that special incentive compensation method and have adopted it for a number of my clients, I should outline how those accounts are established and function.

On occasion, some of my clients have suggested incentivizing their key employees by making them minority owners in the company. That sounds simple but can introduce unwanted problems and complications. A gift of shares is, in the eyes of the IRS, taxable compensation. The key employee then incurs a tax liability with no cash component to use for the payment of those taxes.

In addition, having minority owners in a closely held corporation can result in corporate governance complications; problems due to the death, disability, or either voluntary or involuntary termination of the employee/stockholder; and the resulting need for a complex Stockholders' & Operating Agreement, among other problems.

Also, stock options don't give the employee any current ownership but only the right to buy shares at some future indeterminate time, not usually until there is a liquidation event. As a result, stock options provide only a limited incentive for superior short term performance.

And as also mentioned in the previous chapter, phantom stock makes the employee feel that they are second class citizens which is certainly not the objective of the phantom stock grant. In addition, phantom stock does not provide any easy method for the employee to measure the value of the phantom shares and, therefore, also lacks a short term performance incentive.

To solve some, if not all, of those problems, I developed what I call Equity Capital Accounts. Those accounts act like common stock ownership but without the complications of having minority owners. The Equity Capital Account gives the account holder quarterly allocations, but not payment, for a set percentage of the company's after tax profits plus a participation in any eventual sale of the company or other liquidation event. Because those are allocations and not cash, there is no tax until the account pays a dividend or is converted into a cash return.

As a result of those provisions, the account holder sees the value of their account increase quarterly and has the additional benefit of long term appreciation in the company's enterprise value. In the interim, methods are provided for conversion of a portion, or under certain circumstances all, of the Equity Capital Account into a cash return. The Equity Capital Account then acts as both a short term and long term incentive for superior performance. And because the account holder can lose all or a significant portion of the allocations to their account if they leave the company prematurely, the Equity Capital Account provides "golden handcuffs" or an incentive to remain with the company.

If, for instance, a key employee is given a 4% Equity Capital Account, he or she would have a 4% interest in the after tax earnings of the company. That profit allocation would be credited to the person's Equity Capital Account each quarter, and they are sent a notice of both the current quarter allocation and the total amount in their account.

In the event the company prospers, the owners have the option to declare a dividend or distribution to the account holders. This distribution would convert a portion of each person's Equity Capital Account into a cash bonus.

In the event that an employee with an Equity Capital Account leaves the company, the balance in their Account would be distributed to them according to the following:

- On retirement, all of the Account balance would be paid to the retiring holder but would be paid usually in equal amounts over four or five years.

- If the employee leaves prematurely, they would be paid a portion, usually one-half or three-quarters of their Account balance if they do not subsequently complete with the company but none if they join a competitor.

- If the employee dies or is disabled, they or their heirs would be paid the entire Account balance as with retirement.

- In any event, when an Account holder is no longer with the company, their profit allocations cease.

- In the event that the company is sold or there is some other liquidating event, the Account holder would be paid from the proceeds of the liquidation either the balance in their Account plus their percentage interest in the net proceeds from the liquidation minus what is paid from their Account or their proportionate share of the liquidation proceeds if those proceeds are not sufficient to retire all of the Equity Capital Accounts.

As outlined in the chart on page 177, there are significant advantages to the Equity Capital Accounts that are not enjoyed by other forms of employee incentives. As a result, such accounts should be considered by most companies seeking a method of incentivizing their key managers.

179

Chapter 73 - More Learning from the Mistakes of Others

This book has included many examples of learning from the mistakes of others. Now let's once again, take a look at some of the mistakes clients of mine have made and see if we might learn from, rather than repeat, them.

Some time ago, I told one of my clients, "You purchased an expensive piece of manufacturing equipment for $12 million but then never turned it on." How could that happen? It's easy. It wasn't a piece of equipment, although the result was the same. It was excess and unused working capital. My client had about $12 million of working capital and book value but needed only a fraction of that.

It's always good to have adequate funds, including some reserves, to operate your business and support its liabilities as they come due. It is, however, not good to have an excess that you are not using to generate revenues and profits. After all, you might apply that excess, as well as unused borrowing power, to support your company's growth. You might invest in opening a new territory or market, or in an acquisition of a smaller competitor, or in a development that enhances your product or service.

With unused working capital or borrowing power, your company is suffering from "lost opportunity cost", that is the return on investment that the unused funds could otherwise generate. Be cautious, to some extent be risk adverse, but not to excess. Review your company's balance sheet for unused assets and, to the extent possible, put those assets to productive purposes. Your success should be measured more by your company's growth in revenues and profits than by the amount of its book value. Don't forget, its enterprise value will be based on its profits, not on its stockholders' equity.

Business owners are usually pleased with high levels of working capital and book value but rarely consider that those financial criteria could be too high. If they are, that is an enviable position. Not using the excess, however, is a waste of your company's resources.

Here's another look at some operating mistakes that could or should be avoided.

Some years ago, I had a client who's company manufactured a specialty line of sports equipment. The owner was particularly proud that he had been asked to manufacture a line of women's purses out of a material he used for his sporting goods. Those ladies purses were going to represent a significant contributor to his operations, revenues, and profits.

I didn't like the idea and explained to my client (1) that he knew nothing about women's purses or that market, (2) that he would not control any aspect of the business other than the manufacturing, and (3) that the purse work would detract from the time he should devote to his sports line. No! He wanted the additional revenues and the manufacturing process for the purses would be simpler than those for his sporting goods.

It turned out that the woman for whom he was manufacturing the purses didn't know enough about that market either. The purses didn't sell in the volumes expected, and my client ended up with a significant uncollectable account, excess and worthless inventories of various purse parts, and a large loss rather than the anticipated profits.

My client and I then developed a detailed five year Strategic Plan for expanding his sports equipment line. He followed that plan, the company prospered, and the resulting revenue and profit growth far exceeded what the purses would ever have contributed.

The lesson: Know what business you are in and concentrate on that business. Stick to your core competencies and your company will be successful.

Chapter 74 - Accounting Rules
(For Managers not for Accountants)

At the risk of being redundant, you might be interested in my Accounting Rules. Although this list is certainly not exhaustive, it should be a good start.

- First and most important, design your financial statements for control purposes, not for accountants by accountants.

- If your monthly financial statements are not complete by the 20th of each month, they are an historical curiosity, not a control tool.

- Add a column for the percent of revenue for each line item.

- Budget quarterly using a rolling twelve month system. Then you are then never looking at projections which are more than three months old.

- Your financial statements cannot be used to control expenses unless they are given to each department manager. You can't control what you can't measure.

- Determine which expenses are controllable and which are not; concentrate on those that are.

- Use profit center accounting for all discrete sources of revenue wherever possible and tie bonuses to each profit center's performance.

- Divide expenses by department and tie bonuses to the ratio of departmental expenses to revenue.

- Determine which expenses are Fixed, Semi-Variable, and Variable, then use that information to reduce expenses and increase profits.

- Check make-or-buy and supply-or-subcontract decisions no less than twice a year.

- Combine small line items with related expenses; a $5 million annual revenue company should not show a $500 line item.

- To reduce the number of line items, combine non-controllable expenses with related controllable expenses. For instance, you shouldn't care about the level of payroll taxes; total employee compensation is what is important.

- Notes to individual line items which are in unusual amounts, have unusual fluctuations, or are nonrecurring should be a part of the financial statements.

- Put nonrecurring expenses below the Operating Income line but before the Net Income line.

- An analysis of your Balance Sheet is as important as your Income Statement; understand what the Balance Sheet is telling you.

182

- Your Cash Flow Analysis is as important as your Balance Sheet. Have the accounting department generate it monthly together with the Income Statement and the Balance Sheet. Know what activities are generating cash and which are depleting cash

- Learn what the Cash Flow Analysis is telling you.

- Report and control annual inventory turns, accounts receivable aging, and payables aging.

- Calculate and track the trend for your Labor Efficiency Ratio (Net Revenues divided by Direct Labor) every month.

- Devoting cash to support past due receivables depletes your cash availability; your company is not a bank.

- A company with excess working capital is not making full use of its assets.

- A company with low debt and high book value is not making full use of its financial strength.

- A monthly Cash Flow Analysis is as important as the Income Statement and Balance Sheet, know what activities are generating cash and which are depleting cash.

- Don't let profits hide negative cash flow. Cash is like blood, when it stops flowing, you're dead.

- Some data can and should be reported weekly; determine which and develop that reporting format.

That's all for this list.

183

Chapter 75 - Internet Website Rules

The Internet and Social Media have changed forever the way the world does business. Regardless of your markets, your products or services, or your geographic reach, you need a website and perhaps exposure on one or more Social Media sites. And a good presence is not good enough; it should be one that gives your company a competitive advantage and contributes to its direct sales. In that regard, I've compiled some simple Internet Website rules. Go to your company's website and check it for each of these:

- You company's website should be easy to read and understand. Make sure it's not cluttered. On the homepage there should be a brief description of your company's products and services. In a few words, tell the world what your company is, what it sells, who should be an interested buyer, and why.

- A link to your company's contact information should be on the homepage and also easy to find from any section of the website.

- Contact information should include appropriate individuals with phone, cell phone, e-mail, and physical addresses.

- Your website should be easy to navigate. From the homepage, make it easy to find the right section, product, or service and go to it with a single click. A keyword "Search" feature is always helpful.

- Make sure that every page can be printed and that the printed page can then be read. Some people still like hard copy that can be saved and read without a magnifying glass. Items in pop-up windows usually cannot be printed at all.

- Where appropriate, add video clips to explain product or service uses, applications, and operations. Those will appeal to the video-centric experience of younger managers.

- Make your website interactive. Most of the current generation and all of the coming generation will want the ability on your website to order products or services, check on order status, and both find and communicate with the appropriate person at your company for their specific needs.

- In some cases, it may be valuable to add password accessed website sections for individual customers to show project progress among other customer specific information.

- Provide appropriate downloads such as instruction booklets, procedure manuals, and individual product or service brochures.

- If your company sells spare parts, provide equipment schematics that can be used to easily find, identify, and order needed parts.

184

- If your company sells accessories, show and explain the use of each one. Include an order "Cart" for an easy purchase of those accessories.
- Your website should be updated frequently, checked for search keyword placements, and kept fresh.
- Be sure that all e-mailed questions are answered quickly.
- Migrate and present a summary of your website on multiple mobile devices and social media sites. Internet accesses on a PC is no longer enough. On your next elevator ride, just look at the number of people searching for, and reading, Internet items on their smart phone,
- A Facebook page is no substitute for a captive website.
- Depending upon your markets, consider a "Spanish Option" button on your homepage.

Your website is one of your most important communication tools and should directly connect your company with its customers, promote its products and services, and make buying those both quick and easy. Your website should be one of the most comprehensive in your market area and a direct contributor to your company's sales and profits.

185

Chapter 76 - Non-Financial Criteria

Several times in previous chapters, I have discussed the use of monthly financial statements as control tools. I've also said that you can't control what you can't (or don't) measure. There may be, however, a number of non-financial criteria that you can, and probably should, use to also control your operations and improved your company's profitability and growth. In addition, many of these can be monitored weekly or even daily to provide you, your key managers, and your other employees with an interim measure of performance between the monthly income statements and balance sheets.

Some of these important non-financial criteria, including some that are based on the company's financial statements, are:

- Days in Accounts Receivable or your average accounts receivable collection period. That key factor effecting cash flow is calculated as total accounts receivable divided by total annual revenues with the result of that calculation multiplied by 365.

- Inventory Turns per Year or the level of your inventory compared with your material sales. That metric is calculated as the net revenues from material sales divided by the inventory level.

- Labor Efficiency Ratio or how well you are using the available time for production or the delivery of services. That ratio is calculated as revenue divided by direct labor costs.

- Current Ratio or a measure of your ability to honor your short term liabilities as they come due. That is the total current assets divided by the total current liabilities.

- Return on Total Assets or how efficiently you are using the value of your assets to increase your company's level of profits. That calculation is simply net profits before taxes divided by total assets.

- Another similar metric is Return on Stockholders' Equity or the application of that equity to your company's growth. That ratio is calculated by your net profits before taxes divided by your stockholders' equity or book value.

And of course, different criteria are important for different types of business operations. In Chapter 63, for instance, I mentioned an incentive plan to be used by a CPA firm. In that case, we found that it was the relationship between the hours available to be billed and the actual hours billed that was a particularly significant element in that operation. We used that ratio for a quarterly incentive plan and also began to track that key metric.

In a manufacturing environment, it might be important to control the volume of scrap generated in the production of the product. By comparing the

186

revenue from the scrap sales to the product sales revenue and giving that information to the production department weekly, the wasted scrap can be better controlled.

In internet product sales, non-financial criteria are not only available but are also numerous and relatively easy to monitor. Among those are the number of unique site visitors per day, week, or month; the conversion rate of those visitors to buyers; average ticket revenue per sale; internet advertising costs per revenue dollar for various click-through links, ad methods, or ad placements; search word placement results (SEO); and visitor source data.

Other important measures of performance for many operations could include customer reorder rates, customer attrition or growth (lost versus gained), and both the individual order size and the total monthly or yearly billings by customer.

Review your operations to determine what non-financial criteria contribute to your success. Monitor five or six of those and measure which you believe are the most important. You might then establish a bonus plan based on only one or two of the criteria and provide the results to the pertinent departments using as short a measurement period as feasible. You may be surprised by the improved results.

Also, although these are financial criteria, make sure your income statements have a column for percent of revenue. Those percentages allow you to better track trends when individual expense items change dollar amounts.

187

Chapter 77 - Private Company Ownership

While working with numerous closely held private companies, I have on occasion had the principal owners ask about rewarding key employees with a small ownership position or selling them a small number of shares. In most cases, I am opposed to that. Having minor participants in company ownership can introduce a number of complications and problems. Among those, in the case of a gift or a sale below the enterprise value of the shares, are the immediate tax consequences to the ownership recipient for the value of the shares. A gift or bargain sale is recognized by the IRS as a form of bonus or ordinary income. Taxes are then due on the income represented by the share grant or sale but with no liquid funds to pay the taxes.

In addition, for LLCs and Sub-Chapter S corporations, having minority owners other than the founders or principals introduces the problems of K-1 filings and profit distributions to compensate the minority owners for their share of the flow-through taxes applied to the company's earnings but paid by the individual owners. That introduces not only a potential liability for all of the owners, including the minority owners, but also complicates the personal income tax filings by hem all, including, or course, the minority owners.

In addition, the disposition of minority shares in the event of certain employment or corporate changes should also be controlled. Those restrictions on the future transfer of a minority share ownership position should be used to prevent having unaffiliated owners with no liquidity, little if any interest in the business, and no understanding of how or when they can convert their ownership into a cash return. (Also see Chapter 23.)

Also, in most cases, the minority ownership positions have no value. They do not assure that the holder will continue to be employed by the company; they rarely, if ever, pay dividends or distributions other than for the flow-through tax obligations and not always even then; and the minority shares cannot be sold simply because there is no market for such a small equity ownership position. That lack of value removes much or all of the incentive value of the ownership. Although the minority position could have value in the event of a sale of the company or other liquidation event, that value would only come at some indeterminate time and at a dollar amount that cannot be determined until the liquidity event occurs.

Of course, stock options rather than an immediate ownership grant or sale might solve some of those problems. Options, however, are not ownership and, therefore, do not adequately align the interests of the option holder with those of the principal owners. Because stock options in relatively small private companies are rarely exercised prior to a liquidity event, the option holder has no idea of when that might occur. In that regard, they have little interest in the option or potential ownership absent some idea of the timing for receiving a cash return, a time that might, however, never arrive.

As a result of those problems with using private company ownership as a key employee incentive, I developed an alternate structure which I call an Equity Capital Account. (See Chapter 72.) That form of key manager participation gives the account holder most, or even all, of the benefits of ownership without the complications of issuing small amounts of common stock to other than the company founders or principals. The Equity Capital Accounts can also offer short term distributions combined with long term incentives related to a liquidity event but eliminate the early period tax problems for the holder which would be associated with equity grants.

Private company ownership should be restricted to those employees who are intimately related to the company, have a long term commitment to its operations, are in a position to exercise some measure of control over its future corporate governance, and can understand both the value of that ownership over time and the responsibilities to the c

ompany that it represents.

189

Is This Any Way to Run a Company?   H. Lee Rust

Chapter 78 - Fraud

Although infrequent, over my thirty plus years as a corporate finance consultant, I have had four or five clients lose their companies due to fraud. The classic and most frequent type is a comptroller who sets up several shell companies and then buys phantom goods and services from those operations owned by him or her. I also had a client with an employee who, posing as a company officer, opened credit accounts at a number of retail stores. Using those accounts, he then purchased gift cards for customers who did not exist, gift cards that eventually totaled over $100,000.

Some years ago, I had a client who wondered how her accounting manager could afford a new Ferrari. When she learned the answer, it was too late; her company collapsed. Among other instances of fraud losses, for any company which produces salable scrap, controls need to be in place to make sure all of the receipts from scrap sales are deposited in the company account.

There are other simple precautions you can also use to guard your corporate assets and minimize, if not eliminate, fraud losses. First, require two signatures for all company checks. Even if you are the sole owner in your company and the only check signer, add another required signature. Those should include you plus either one of two additional approved signers. That check signing procedure makes forgery more difficult and lets others know that you are checking on the use and application of company funds.

In addition, at least once every two or three months, you should ask for a copy of your company's general ledger and review that raw data line by line. By questioning any entries with names you don't recognize, you let your accounting personnel know that you are looking. Others in your company will also learn that they may be asked about any suspect withdrawals. As another precaution, you should also ask to review the last few months of company credit card invoices, another prime area for fraud.

For an additional control procedure, set up a system of written purchase requisitions. Any item or service to be purchased by your company should be requested on a formal, written, purchase requisition with one or two approval signatures required, depending upon the size of the requisition. Of course, no one in the accounting department should also approve a purchase requisition. The buying function should be well separated from the payment function.

And previously, I've mentioned the value of having your company's annual financial statements audited. Although more expensive than a review or compilation, an audit is the "Good Housekeeping Seal of Approval" as to your accounting procedures and internal controls. Audits are not designed specifically to find or prevent fraud, but they help and, again, put all on notice that an independent auditor will be looking.

190

Finally, it is an excellent practice to have a written Accounting Procedure Manual. That Manual should cover each of your company's accounting methods and all internal costs and accounting controls. Buy some fraud insurance, not from an insurance company but by establishing your own internal controls. It's easy to do, cost you little, and could save your company from a horrendous and perhaps fatal loss.

191

Is This Any Way to Run a Company?   H. Lee Rust

Chapter 79 - More Learning from Others

Let's take an additional look at some the mistakes clients of mine have made and, again, see if we might learn from, rather than repeat, them.

Back in the 1980's, I had a client with a Florida same-day delivery service. In order to promote that, he developed a credit card activated mailing machine. It weighted the package, charged the client's credit card, and accepted the delivery through a secure chute. After seeing his prototype, I realized the potential of that device and urged my client to find a partner large enough to sell the machines and put them in every post office in the U.S. Pitney Bowes, FedEx, and the United States Postal Service were each interested.

No, he wanted to promote his same-day delivery service and refused to consider taking on a senior partner who could and would realize the potential of his idea. He wanted to keep it all for himself and not share the returns with anyone else.

Back when I worked in corporate finance with a stock brokerage firm, I heard it said that pigs get fattened, but hogs get slaughtered. What happened? Developing the mailing machine ate up all the company's working capital, the little same-day delivery service (competing with FedEx overnight) failed, and my client ended up with nothing. Meanwhile, some other company created an automated mailing machine and has put them in post offices throughout the country.

The lesson: If you have a great idea but not enough money to develop it, find a partner with the money and give up some of the returns. Don't be a hog!

Another lesson from this example: Know what business you're in and stick to what you know. My client was in the package delivery service not the machinery development, manufacture, and sales business.

Back in about 1985, I started working with a client in a high-tech product development and production company. He was a long-term participant and leader in his field and had already built and sold one company in his area of expertise. Over the years, I helped him buy several smaller subsidiary operations and sell one of his more mature divisions. I also worked with him on Strategic Planning and reviewing at least two acquisition proposals from much larger companies.

Over time, Mark built his operations to well over $30 million in annual sales and then had five divisions, each with a General Manager. They, however, were more technicians and engineers than managers.

As Mark's age crept into the 70's, I would on occasion suggest that he should have a Succession Plan. There was no one, I told him, then in his company with either the management skills or experience needed to manage his operations without him there on a daily basis. But that was a blind spot for

192

him. He didn't want to hire and train a potential replacement and just wouldn't consider any need for eventually replacing himself even though he was the company.

Then the inevitable happened; Mark died suddenly and left his company without a leader. It drifted; no one seemed to know what to do. An ineffective President was appointed but was neither capable nor qualified. Six months later, Mark's company was gone. Worse yet, his wife had co-signed on all company debts.

The lesson: You need a well thought out, written Succession Plan regardless of your age or the status of your company. You also need someone at the company who is or will be qualified to replace you. Don't neglect this crucial aspect of your company's operations. You've worked hard to build what you have, don't jeopardize that with an unforeseen event that can be so easily be remedied.

Also, succession plans are not only for company principals. They should be in place for each critical management position as well as for particularly hard to replace technical talent.

Chapter 80 - Audit Value

I frequently urge my clients to have their annual financial statements audited. It cost more than a review and certainly more than a simple compilation, but it is well worth the price.

If you ever expect to sell your company to a larger corporate owner, having a history of audited financial statements will increase the price you (or your heirs) might receive. For your company's financial condition, it's the "Good housekeeping Seal of Approval", if you are old enough to remember that iconic phrase. In addition, your bank will often be more willing to extend or expand available credit if they can review annual audits and count on having them in the future.

And for you, as an owner, executive, or advisor, the annual audit certifies that the independent auditor conducted a number of financial tests to verify that the company's balance sheet and income statement accurately reflect its financial condition and past year's performance.

Often relatively small companies only have their internal financial statements "compiled" by their outside CPA. That only means that the accountant took the financials prepared by the company and rewrote them in a more standard format. No verification or financial tests were performed and, certainly, the independent accountant offers no assurance that the statements are accurate.

The next step up is an annual review. For that form of financial reporting, the independent CPA performs certain limited tests but still offers no independent opinion as to the validity of the report.

In an audit, however, the CPA expands the scope of their financial tests and does offer an independent opinion that the statements fairly present the financial condition and performance of the company. That independent opinion is valuable to the company's banker, potential buyers, and owners; valuable enough to justify the added expense of an audit.

In addition, many CPA firms, as a part of their auditing procedures, provide the company owners and top executives with a "Management Letter". That note to the owners and top executives outlines certain items that turned up during the audit work and might be of importance to the company's top executives. Often that Management Letter includes a description of any deficiencies or material weaknesses in the company's financial reporting and internal control procedures that should be corrected. In that regard, the Management Letter can be almost as valuable to the company as the audit report itself.

If your company does not have fully audited financial statements, ask your CPA about the added cost of having annual audits. You will get significant value from that annual expense.

Chapter 81 - Working Capital

Working Capital, defined as current assets minus current liabilities, is a measure of the short term funds available to support your company's day-to-day operations. The Working Capital Ratio or, more frequently, the Current Ratio, is defined as current assets divided by current liabilities. That Current Ratio is an indication of your company's ability to honor its short term obligations as they come due. In either case, the amount of available Working Capital is a measure of your company's liquidity and is a key component of its overall financial health.

By calculating the Working Capital levels held by your company each month and keeping a record at six month intervals over a three to five year period, you can establish that amount of Working Capital that is appropriate for your operations. During an expansion period, you can also use the relationship of Working Capital to annual Revenues to determine how you can comfortably fund that continued growth.

You can also calculate your company's Current Ratio over those same six months intervals and determine a comfortable level for that indicator of financial strength. Although there is certainly no standard for all types of operations and markets, if your company's Current Ratio falls below 1.2 to 1, that is a warning sign that funding your short term future operations could become more difficult.

Fine, so you can calculate Working Capital and your company's Current Ratio. But if those measures of financial strength are deficient, what can you do about it? The principal asset components of Working Capital are cash, accounts receivable, and inventory. The principal liability components are trade payables and expense accruals. Those, of course, are all interrelated. However, by reducing your levels of inventory, you can convert inventory into cash but must be careful that out of stock materials don't adversely affect your production or service functions.

In addition, of course, the level of available cash can be enhanced by increasing profits as well as by reducing the collection period for your accounts receivable. You might also extend your trade payment terms consistent with taking payment discounts and maintaining good relationships with your suppliers. Of all of the above, the best method of increasing the level of Working Capital is increased profitability.

In regard to an understanding of your company's available and needed Working Capital levels, in addition to a deficiency, you can also have too much Working Capital. By holding much higher levels of Working Capital than needed to comfortably fund your company's current operations, you probably have unused assets that might be better reinvested in future growth. That excess can also be used to provide dividends for the company's owners

195

and bonuses to the key individuals who helped generate the high Working Capital level.

You need enough Working Capital and should take measures to assure that you do. If you have too much, determine the best use for the excess. But understand how much Working Capital your company needs and measure it for each accounting period. The majority of company failures are either caused by a Working Capital deficiency or are forecast by a consistent drop in Working Capital levels over time. Don't let either cause your company's operations to falter.

Chapter 82 - Borrowing Capacity

Every corporate owner and executive should have an understanding of their company's borrowing power. At any time an opportunity might suddenly call for more cash than is on hand, some event might deplete reserves or working capital, or continued growth might best be supported with a loan. In any event, it is good to understand borrowing capacity, what factors might affect your ability to quickly raise additional funds, and what factors might decrease that capacity.

I'm not a banker and certainly can't cover all aspects of corporate borrowing, but I can offer the highlights. In that regard, I would like to discuss only two borrowing sources: banks and commercial lenders. Many banks present themselves as "asset based lenders". That is, they lend against the collateral value of the company's tangible assets. Although it is true that the bank wants the value of those assets to fully cover the borrowings, in general, banks are cash flow lenders. They look more to the company's earnings to service the loan than to the liquidation value of the assets.

However, a commercial lender, which is not a bank, is more likely to be a source for a true asset based loan. On occasion, I have even arranged loans from commercial lenders for companies with recent losses but good asset collateral value. But loans from a commercial lender are more expensive than those that a bank might offer. For that reason, I always calculate the total cost of funds, including all fees and expenses, and not only the simple interest rate charged for the loan.

As to borrowing capacity for either a bank loan generally supported by cash flow or a loan from a commercial lender, I usually assume that the company's accounts receivable with reasonably short ageing can support a loan that is about 75% to 80% of the receivables. About 30% to 50% of the finished goods inventory can be used as collateral depending upon the salability of the inventory. Work in process and raw materials are not often used as loan collateral except in rare cases where the raw materials are readily salable. Fixed assets in the form of machinery and equipment usually have low, if any, collateral value, perhaps 10% or less of the cost basis.

Of course, the best source of information regarding your company's borrowing capacity is its bank. In that regard, you should not only provide your bank with your company's monthly financial statements, even if not required, but should also periodically ask their opinion as to your borrowing capacity. Treat your banker as a partner; then when you need additional capital, you will have much less to explain. Both you and your banker will already have many of the answers.

Chapter 83 - Bank Financing

In the previous chapter, we discussed borrowing capacity, and I mentioned both banks and commercial lenders. Now, let's expand on that and talk about applying for financing. Regardless of whether a bank or a commercial lender is the source of the funds, the approach is the same. And as with most corporate endeavors, being thorough is important. That means giving the financing source virtually all of the information they might need or want long before they ask.

I do that with a detailed Corporate Profile & Financing Request. The Corporate Profile segment of that document includes a brief, but fairly complete, description of the borrower. That includes a short history of the company, its corporate structure & ownership, the business in which it participates, and information regarding its products and services, markets, competition, and management. Depending upon the company, it might also be important to describe its suppliers, its facilities and equipment, and its real estate holdings.

There should also be a complete listing of all interest bearing debts owed by the company. For each one, that list should show the name of the lender, the original issuance date and amount of the loan, the current outstanding principal owed, the interest rate and maturity date, and the collateral securing the loan. Of course, it should also show which of the loans will be retired with the proceeds of the refinancing.

Be sure that the descriptive portion of the Profile also outlines any litigation in process, pending, or threatened and discusses any other contingent liabilities that might not be on the balance sheet. Finally, there should be a detailed financial section and, of course, a complete description of the financing being requested.

As to the financial information either a bank or a commercial lender will need, I usually compile a five year income statement history on a single page, if feasible, and with columns for dollars as well as percent of revenues. I also add "Notes to the Financials" which explain certain of the line items. I then use the most recent annual income statement to calculate the debt service coverage based on the financing being requested and also list various covenants that might be requested by the lender with calculations that show the company's compliance with those.

For any loan application, regardless of the potential source of the loan, anticipate the questions the lender might ask and answer them in advance. Do as much work for the lender as feasible, and your financing request will have a greater chance of being accepted.

Chapter 84 - Financing Sources

In the last two chapters, we discussed borrowing capacity and loan applications. I also mentioned both banks and commercial lenders. Now, however, let's talk about other potential financing sources.

Although my experience has taught me that banks and commercial lenders are the principal sources of financing for the great majority of small to medium sized, privately owned companies, there are other sources of capital funds. In most cases, however, those are much more problematic.

Among alternate funding sources, angel investors are frequently mentioned. Those are high net worth individuals that write big checks to participate in risky ventures. For over thirty years, I've heard about those angels but have never met one. They do exist but virtually never invest outside the markets or operations with which they have direct past experience. That severely limits angel investors as an available source of financing for most companies.

As to private equity and venture capital firms, their focus is principally on equity investments with high potential returns in a relatively short period of time. As a result, those capital sources are not generally available to the mundane companies of the world even though their potential return may be as good but are judged by the investors to be too limited.

There is, however, another source of corporate funding that is often used for financing beyond what a bank or commercial lender will provide. That source comes from family and friends. Those are individuals with disposable funds and most often ones that can say, "I don't know anything about your markets or operations, but I know you and will bet on your ability." But in seeking that source of funding, don't forget that family and friends present potential problems that other financing sources don't have. Among others, such related party loans or equity investments can adversely affect future personal relationships.

An often neglected source of capital funding is from non-financial companies which are related to your operations and which might have an indirect interest in seeing that your company succeeds. Those could include your principal suppliers or even your largest customers. However, for funding from any of those sources, the lender or investor must be chosen with care. As a lender or investor in your company, a related company might gain inside information that you would rather not provide. In addition, if the loan or investment does not go as planned, it could also adversely affect a corporate relationship which is important to your future operations.

If your company needs funds, the first rule is to compile a thorough presentation that answers virtually all the questions your funding source might ask. Then carefully pick those sources you judge to be most available and give them your funding request. Then be prepared not only for questions

199

before a loan or investment is made but also for questions and potential problems after the funds have been committed.

In any discussion of financing sources for small to medium sized companies, I would be remiss in not mentioning "croudfunding". Under new Securities & Exchange Commission (SEC) rules the restrictions on soliciting investments from individuals have been substantially relaxed and have spawned a number of websites that purport to assist companies raising such funds.

In general, however, I am opposed to croudfunding. The amounts that can be raised are quite small and are most often less than what a company's needs to support its growth or its operations. In addition, the croudfunding rules, although relaxed, are still complex. But of most importance, it is not advisable for any small to midsized company to have a large number of minor investors all of whom have only a tenuous relationship to the company and its operations. Those unrelated investors can present future problems and require future attention that absorb executive time better spent on the company itself.

If a company has sufficient size and potential to become publicly owned through an IPO (Initial Public Offering), that option is a good one. But a much smaller company should not convert itself into a quasi publicly owned company with many of the disadvantages of that public ownership and few, if any, of the advantages.

200

Chapter 85 - The Final Chapter

You won't live forever, so plan accordingly. Even though I intend to work until I'm at least a hundred years old, I also understand that might not be possible. Others would like to retire at some point well before that or may find that they can't continue to work due to health or other problems. And any of your company's managers, including you, may receive an offer from another company they can't refuse or may have to relocate for other reasons.

Regardless of the reasons, there's always some turnover in the personnel in any company. With all of your planning, plan for those changes, particularly at the management levels. Every manager should have identified a person who could fill their job on either a temporary or permanent basis and have begun to train that person to do that. (Also see Chapters 13 and 43.) In the event a department is too small to have that management depth, there should still be someone, perhaps from another department, who could take over in an emergency.

Training successors and the transfer of management responsibilities between generations is an integral part of good management. Otherwise, you may suddenly find a vacuum in a key position that causes serious problems. And the higher the management position, the more important your succession planning will be.

This is particularly true where company ownership is concerned. In a small, single owner company, the death or disability of the owner and principal executive can result in the death of the company itself. I've seen it happen on more than one occasion. Where any significant ownership is a factor, it's advisable to not only plan for the management succession but also for the disposition of the equity in the event the stockholder is no longer employed, dies, or is disabled. Otherwise, uninvolved heirs to private company ownership too often become an impediment to its remaining managers.

Those heirs may not understand why the company doesn't pay dividends, can't repurchase their ownership interest, or values that ownership at a price they consider too low. Rather than impose the "stockholder from hell" on a closely held company which has just lost a key executive, it's much better to have established in advance how both management succession and the disposition of the equity will be handled.

In regard to such stockholder agreements and equity repurchase obligations, it may also be advisable to consider life insurance covering the individual stockholders with the proceeds pledged to the company's stock repurchase obligations. (Also see Chapter 23.) This can not only prevent a capital drain due to the death of a stockholder but can also provide a cash return to the stockholder's heirs which might not otherwise be available from the company. On numerous occasions over the years, I've drafted the basic terms and conditions for various stockholder agreements and always include both pricing formulas and payment terms for the equity of any employee stockholder who is no longer employed for any reason.

Don't make the health of your company dependent on the health of any one of its executives. Succession planning, generational transfers of management responsibility, and the disposition of company ownership should all be discussed and agreed well before any need is suddenly thrust on the company and its other managers.

In this book, I've enjoyed talking with you about each of the various management topics we've covered. As both you and your company develop, I hope they will be helpful. And each time you ask "Is this any way to run a company?", I also hope the answer and the topics covered in this book make any changes both more appropriate and more productive. Also, don't forget that corporate management is more art than science so practice the art and choose what you believe is best for you, your company, and its operations. The art of management can and should be fun as well as profitable.

202

Index

N

nepotism - 76-78

nominal cash flow - 57

noncompetition agreements - 141, 147, 161

non-financial criteria - 186-187

non-solicitation agreements - 141, 147

O

occupancy costs - 16, 55, 120

Operating Agreements - 174, 178

operations audits - 36, 166

organization charts - 23, 36, 37, 79-80, 116, 117, 151, 161

organization, personal - 155-156

outsourcing - 157-159, 161

ownership transfers - 37-38

P

partnership(s) - 48, 58, 81, 87, 88, 106, 174

penalties - 44, 95, 96, 165

PEO (Professional Employer Organizations) - 129

performance reviews - 92-94, 129, 151

Peter Principal - 22-24, 143

phantom stock, 62

policy handbook - 160-162

preferred stock - 37-38

pricing - 8, 18, 52, 70-71, 132, 143, 157, 161, 168, 202

print media - 34

procedure manuals - 14, 129, 160-162, 184, 191

product placement marketing - 32

profit centers - 9, 10, 17, 18, 52, 70, 129, 171, 182

profitability - 8, 17-18, 48, 81, 103, 186, 195

project cost accounting - 18

projections, financial, 30, 54-56, 68, 79, 82, 88, 101, 114, 132, 169

public company - 41, 122-124

public offerings - , 40, 42, 123, 131, 170, 200

Q

quality control - 45, 161

R

real estate - 66, 88, 142, 165, 198

receptionists 11-12

recruiters, executive - 73

reputation, corporate, 19, 90-91, 135, 157, 158

risk management - 128-130, 153, 160, 161

S

sales and marketing - 19-21, 28, 32-34, 51, 52

sales calls - 20, 85, 145, 146

sales cycle - 20

sales manager - 7-9, 20, 23, 71, 80, 144 -146

sales methods - 20

sales representatives - 20, 85, 144-146

salespeople -9, 19, 21, 23, 28, 33, 71, 85, 90, 104, 141, 144, 168

Sarbanes-Oxley - 41, 42, 123

SEC (Securities and Exchange Commission) - 111, 133, 170, 200

semi-variable costs - 55, 69

setting prices - 8, 18, 52, 70-71, 132, 143, 157, 161, 168, 202

www.ingramcontent.com/pod-product-compliance
Lightning Source LLC
Chambersburg PA
CBHW031930190326
41519CB00007B/476